Hoʻokupu

AN OFFERING OF LITERATURE

Ho'okupu
AN OFFERING OF LITERATURE

by
Native Hawaiian Women

❦ EDITED BY ❦
MIYOKO SUGANO AND JACKIE JOHNSON

❦ ASSISTED BY ❦
CAROL SEVERANCE AND KU'ULEI KEPA'A

MUTUAL PUBLISHING

ISBN-10: 1-56647-902-9
ISBN-13: 978-1-56647-902-8

Library of Congress Cataloging-in-Publication Data
Ho'okupu : an offering of literature / by native Hawaiian women ; edited by Miyoko Sugano and Jackie Johnson ; assisted by Carol Severance and Ku'ulei Kepa'a.
    p. cm.
  ISBN 1-56647-902-9 (softcover : alk. paper)
  1. American literature--Hawaii. 2. Women--Hawaii--Literary collections. 3. American literature--Women authors. 4. Hawaii--Literary collections. I. Sugano, Miyoko.
  PS571.H3H66 2009
  810.8"09969--dc22
                    2009015571

Cover illustration by Esther Szegedy

Design by Kyle Higa

First Printing June 2009

Mutual Publishing, LLC
1215 Center Street, Suite 210
Honolulu, Hawai'i 96816
Ph: 808-732-1709 / Fax: 808-734-4094
email: info@mutualpublishing.com
www.mutualpublishing.com

Printed in Korea

Table of Contents

Acknowledgments

GRATEFUL ACKNOWLEDGMENT IS MADE FOR PERMISSION TO REPRINT THE
FOLLOWING WORKS:

Coochie Cayan, "Blue waves swell to shore," and "All around we see" from her
"Haikus For the Days of the Voyaging Canoes." Reprinted from *'Ōiwi: A Native
Hawaiian Journal, II.*

Coochie Cayan, "Braddah." Reprinted from *Westwinds'94* (University of Hawai'i-
West O'ahu, 1994).

Coochie Cayan, "Pele's Last Rainforest." Reprinted from *La'ila: An Anthology of the
Women's Center Reading Series I* (Special Issue of *Kaimana: Literary Arts Hawai'i*,
Special Issue, 1996).

Cathy Kanoelani Ikeda, "Max Was Hea." Reprinted from *Growing Up Local: an
anthology of poetry and prose from Hawai'i*, edited by Eric Chock, James R. Harstad,
Darrell H.Y. Lum & Bill Teeter (Honolulu: Bamboo Ridge Press, 1998).

Victoria Nalani Kneubuhl, "Ho'oulu Lāhui." Reprinted from *The Quietest Singer*,
edited by Darrell H.Y. Lum, Joseph Stanton, and Estelle Enoki (State Foundation
on Culture and the Arts, 2000).

Mahealani Perez-Wendt, "Compassionate Hina," "Calvary at 'Anaeho'omalu,"
"Uluhaimalama," "Native Hawaiian in Prison" (retitled "Blue Light"), "Queenie,"
and "My Bus Is Two Hours Late." Reprinted from *Uluhaimalama* (Kuleana 'Ōiwi
Press, 2007).

Tamara Wong-Morrison, "Strange Scent." Reprinted from *Bamboo Ridge #25*
(Honolulu: Bamboo Ridge Press, Fall 1983).

Foreword
Nā Wāhine Hawaiʻi

We, Nā Wāhine Hawaiʻi, are Goddesses, dwelling in the spiritual realm of the living. Our analytic scale navigates towards the ethereal allowing us to see that which exists behind our eyelids. Searching our umauma to understand what was and will always be. This search takes us to the island of Lehua, where we deposit our bones in Papa and follow the trail of souls, timeless souls, out beyond the reach of sight and sound to horizons, kahiki kū, kahiki moe.

We observe the islands as the ʻiwa does. We mingle with the gods of our ancestors. Our loved ones swarm our dreams and feed our souls. They remind us to give offerings to our gods, visit the place of our birth, bathe in the sands of Moʻomomi, feel the downpour of the rainforest, drink in the scent of ʻawapuhi, learn from those we love, stand firmly on our land and then chant from the depths of our soul, "He Hawaiʻi au."

When we return to reclaim our bones, our naʻau regurgitate in feeble words the wisdom gained between ka lā hiki and ka lā kau. The fundamental truth to our existence is that our foundation is set to stand the test of time, a gift of ancestral blood from one generation to the next. We are the stabilizing factor of our Hawaiian universe, we pass the ipu of definiteness full of love, passion, strength, artistic imagery, protective instincts and innate family desires.

We, Nā Wāhine Hawaiʻi, know the path between kahiki kū, kahiki moe to refresh our passion and desires to write again the songs and stories of our lives and to take our place in the loʻi of Hāloa. ʻAmama, ua noa, lele wale aku nō!

This book is a gift from us, Nā Wāhine Hawaiʻi, to the next generation. The book can teach only if you are ready to learn about who you are and where you are in the time and place of our cyclic existence.

᠊ᢀ Pualani Kanakaʻole Kanahele

NOTES FOR NĀ WĀHINE HAWAIʻI PROVIDED BY PUALANI KANAKAʻOLE KANAHELE

ʻAMAMA, UA NOA:	The prayer is done, the kapu is over; the closing of prayer.
LELE WALE AKU NŌ:	It (prayer) has flown. An assurance that it was gone and flew to the entities of the places for which it was intended.
HĀLOA:	The progenitor of the Hawaiian race, whose brother was the kalo and whose name is the kānāwai for sustaining our blood flow; literally means 'long breath.'
HE HAWAIʻI AUʻ:	I am Hawaiian!
ʻIWA:	Frigate bird which is capable of flying the length of the Hawaiian archipelago.
KAHIKI KŪ:	The pillars of sunrise on the eastern horizon.
KAHIKI MOE:	The pillars of sunset on the western horizon.
KA LĀ HIKI:	The place where the sun enters, sunrise.
KA LĀ KAU:	The place where the sun sets, sunset.
LEHUA ISLAND:	A volcanic tuff north of the island of Niʻihau and west of the island of Kauaʻi, the icon of the sunset, the end of the day or the end of life; a place where the spirit leaves for places unknown.
UMAUMA:	Chest, the place which resonates the cadence of life.

Mele Hoʻokipa

Aia ka meaʻai i ka awāwa
i ke kai, ika hale laʻa o Pele
i ka wao nahele.
Inā hāmama nō ka ʻumeke
Alaila, e hoʻopihapiha me ka mea ola!

> The food is in the valley,
> in the sea, in the sacred house of Pele
> in the forest.
> If the calabash is indeed open
> Then fill it with life-giving substance!

—Pualani Kanakaʻole Kanahele

Ke Kāhea

(GREETINGS)

This anthology, a ho'okupu, is a gift from many women writers: teachers in the public, charter, and private schools, professors from the University of Hawai'i, lawyers, social workers, secretaries, students, kumu hula—teachers of hula and chant, coming from different parts of the state: O'ahu, Moloka'i, the island of Hawai'i; and also from the continental U.S.

These writers, with their love and knowledge of the Hawaiian language and all that it enables them to think and express, have willingly contributed their chants, mele, poems, stories and a play in English. That they have written in English is not a sign of adaptation or accommodation. They have, as Connie Fife, a Native American, says, "transformed a medium once used to oppress and silence us [indigenous people] so that we might dwindle away without resistance. We have found that the written word does not have to be wrapped in the thoughts of the colonizer, but rather can convey the resilience of our survival." [1]

Albert Wendt, internationally recognized Samoan novelist, speaking about Pacific Islanders writing in English, explains the use of English by indigenous people in this way: "We have indigenized and enriched the language of the colonizers and used it to declare our independence and uniqueness; to analyze colonialism itself and its effects upon us; to free ourselves of the mythologies created about us in colonial literature." [2]

They speak as Hawaiians, but they also speak as individuals. Each writer reveals her own view of Hawaiian culture and Hawaiians and the conflict of Hawaiians with the outside forces, usually the colonizers either directly, indirectly, or obliquely. Most of the works are in English, a few are in Hawaiian and in English. The varieties of English range from Standard (American) English to "Pidgin" as the local people refer to what the linguists label as Hawai'i Creole English (HCE). Each writer has chosen the language appropriate for her subject, her purpose and

---

[1] Connie Fife. Introduction. *The Colour of Resistance: A Contemporary Collection of Writing by Aboriginal Women.* Ed. by Connie Fife, 2.
[2] Wendt, Albert. Introduction. *Nuanua: Pacific Writing in English Since 1980.* Ed. by Albert Wendt, 3.

theme and her point of view. In terms of orthography, the spelling of Hawaiian words, using or not using features such as ʻokina, glottal stop marked by the inverted apostrophe, or the kahakō, a macron indicating a lengthening of a vowel, has followed the style of the particular writer. The same is true for italicizing Hawaiian words and thus treating them as foreign words. The widest orthographic variation has to do with the "Pidgin" since there is no agreed upon orthography. Some of these writers chose to more closely imitate the speech sound, others confined "Pidgin" use to selected phrases.

Mahalo

Mahalo nui loa to the many Native Hawaiian women writers who responded to our call for submissions of their work to appear in this public and print world with eagerness and enthusiasm. Also thanks to videographer Esther Figueroa of Juniroa Productions in Honolulu for sharing with us "The Birth of Moʻomomi" which she videotaped in Molokaʻi. We are particularly grateful to Pualani Kanakaʻole Kanahele for providing the opening chant and Nalanianakaʻole for providing the closing chant.

Mahalo also to the assistance provided by Carol Severance, playwright, short story writer and novelist, who poured over many submissions to help us make the difficult choice of selections and read over a number of drafts of the anthology. A special mahalo to Kuʻulei Kepaʻa for resurrecting the anthology lost in Sugano's mildewed floppy disks by word processing the document in its entirety from her hard copy and for proofreading it for Hawaiian and English errors. A graduate of UHH with a major in English and a minor in Hawaiian Studies, she is a program support specialist for the Kahuawaiola Indigenous Teacher Education Program of Ka Haka ʻUla O Keʻelikōlani College of Hawaiian Language at the University of Hawaiʻi at Hilo.

Others who helped us to maintain the integrity in the use of the Hawaiian language include the late Haunani Bernardino, Associate Professor of Hawaiian/Hawaiian Studies, and Larry Kimura, Assistant Professor of Hawaiian/Hawaiian Studies, both of the Ka Haka ʻUla O Keʻelikōlani College of Hawaiian Language at the University of Hawaiʻi at Hilo.

We extend our gratitude also to Junko Nowaki, recently retired as the public services librarian in charge of the Hawaiian Collection for UHH, for sharing her knowledge and her willingness to help locate many essential materials; Susan Yugawa, graphic artist at the Graphics Department of the UHH library, for her advice and patience; Carole Kuba and Cathy Gourd of the Humanities Division office staff, College of Arts and Sciences at UHH who took care of various details, even helping pull Sugano out of the word processing quagmire that she fell into from time to time.

Special thanks from Miyoko Sugano to her students in Eng. 394K: Native Hawaiian Women Writers in Spring, 1997, for their enthusiastic, critical and sensitive efforts in commenting on the early draft of this anthology used as a text and for interviewing their "adopted" writers. A few of their interviews appear in the Appendix.

—Miyoko Sugano, Emeritus Professor of English at UH Hilo
—Jackie Pualani Johnson, Professor of Theatre Arts at UHH

Ka Waiho A Ka Manaʻo

❧ Haunani Bernardino ☙

‘O ka lau o ke kāwelu
Hiehie i ka naue ‘ana a‘e
Noho ‘ia maila e ka ua
Me ke ‘ala ‘awapuhi onaona

The kāwelu
Bends gracefully in movement,
Embraced by rain
And the fragrant scent of ginger.

E ka mea nolu ehu o ka nahele
I laila e la‘i ai ka ‘i‘ini
‘Ike ‘ia ka waiho a ka mana‘o
‘Ano ‘ai wale ka nohona iho

Oh, soft one of the forest
It is there that all yearning is calmed,
Where deepest thoughts are shared
With warmth and love.

Hoa pili ‘oe i ka pono
A he kuleana kou i ‘ane‘i
‘A‘ohe lua e like ai
Me ke aloha a kāua i honi ai

True and kind friend
You will always be near
For nothing could ever compare
To the tenderness with which we kissed.

Hāmākua

✺ KANANI ATON ✺

Immense ʻulu tree
Tall, striking against the sky
Fruit sags delicious

Hana i ka loʻi [1]

✺ KANANI ATON ✺

Cool pebbles of rain
Fall laughing on taro leaves
Wish I knew the joke

---

[1] work in the taro patch

Kona Bliss
(for ckhy)

❧ PHYLLIS COOCHIE CAYAN ☙

*

Hāʻukeʻuke
cling to rocks awash in waves,
     like your warm embrace.

***

Hāpuna

❧ KANANI ATON ☙

Silence on the beach
I swim strongly toward sunset
Ancient whales singing

"Blue waves" FROM "Haikus for the Days of the Voyaging Canoes"

❧ PHYLLIS COOCHIE CAYAN ❧

Blue waves swell to shore,
The kōlea leaves footprints,
Petroglyphs in sand.

Ka ʻIolani

❧ Kanani Aton ❧

He swims skyward and
    stretches a majestic wing span to
        search the verdant, steep pali of Waipiʻo once
        more.

Brown speckled body, light-tipped wings lift in
    the salt mist air.
He floats, drifts on unseen currents with
    sharp, instinctual eyes
        they glitter

        Suddenly,
        thick muscular legs tucked underneath
        plumage of flying color he comes cascading
        down.

He disappears behind the sharp cliff and
I hear his victorious cry resound in the steep walls.

"All around" FROM "Haikus for the Days of the Voyaging Canoes"

ॐ PHYLLIS COOCHIE CAYAN ☙

All around we see
Deep blue water meet the sky
Merging their mana.

**

Compassionate Hina

⚘ MAHEALANI PEREZ-WENDT (FORMERLY KAMAUU) ⚘

I have bathed in moonlight
And guided lover's hands
over breasts soft and round;
Known the sweet winds of Hina,
Turned to hear the rustle
Of forbidden gardens
And gone beyond.

Compassionate Hina—
A haloed angel sings
Light and holy,
Petaled and sweet
Fragile as gardenia.

I have bathed in moonlight
And guided lover's hands;
I have known Hina
with hands, breast, heart,
Seed.

Ke Ahi 'Ālapa Kūkulu 'Ula I Ka Lani

⁓ NALANIKANAKA'OLE ⟱

Ke ahi 'ālapa kūkulu 'ula i ka lani
Imi a'ela i pohā mai ka māwae
I 'ena'ena nā wao lehua o Puna ē
Ke 'ā ho'olapa a lau i ke kai

Ke nome 'owē ke ka'a 'owē
Pōpo'i Kapa'ahu pōpo'i 'Ōhi'a
I ke kai o Hō'ea i ka uka o Kia'i

Lapakū ka Wahine 'ai lehua
Hō'ike ana lā'au kuahulu i ka pō
Nene'e momoku i ka papalauahi
Hanu'u a'ela i ka pu'u o Kupaianaha

Ke nome 'owē ke ka'a 'owē
Pōpo'i Kapa'ahu pōpo'i 'Ōhi'a
I ke kai o Hō'ea i ka uka o Kia'i

Kū ē ka nalu nui ha'i i ke one I
Ke one kaulana i nā niu moe
Lau ka pāhoehoe kīpuni mai ke kai
Kūnou mai ka niu ha'a i ka Wahine ē

Ke nome 'owē ke ka'a 'owē
Pōpo'i Kapa'ahu pōpo'i 'Ōhi'a
I ke kai o Hō'ea i ka uka o Kia'i

Ke ʻā kaʻalolohi ke iho nei ke kai
Ke ʻā noho waʻawaʻa ke iho nei ke kai
I eieieiei

Ke nome ʻowē ke kaʻa ʻowē
Pōpoʻi Kapaʻahu pōpoʻi ʻŌhiʻa
I ke kai o Hōʻea i ka uka o Kiaʻi

He inoa no HiʻiakaikapolioPele.

A Red Fire Column Blazes High Into the Heavens

❧ NALANIKANAKA'OLE ☙

A red fire column blazes high into the heavens
Searching to burst at the fissure
Glowing brightly are the lehua forests of Puna
Fiery ridges that flame to the sea

The rustling lava the rolling lava
Kapa'ahu is covered 'Ōhi'a is covered
At the sea of Hō'ea to the uplands of Kia'i

The woman that consumes lehua erupts in passion
At night shows feathery flames from tree trunks
Moving and breaking off from the flowing magma
From the hill of Kupaianaha the ebbing lava

The rustling lava the rolling lava
Kapa'ahu is covered 'Ōhi'a is covered
At the sea of Hō'ea to the uplands of Kia'i

Standing waves break on the sands of I
The celebrated land of the low lying palms
Rounding the point a finger of lava advances
The low lying palms bow in honor of the woman

The rustling lava the rolling lava
Kapa'ahu is covered 'Ōhi'a is covered
At the sea of Hō'ea to the uplands of Kia'i

The slow moving fires gives course to the sea
The dwelling furrows gives course to the sea
The low churning fires gives course to the sea

The rustling lava the rolling lava
Kapaʻahu is covered ʻŌhiʻa is covered
At the sea of Hōʻea to the uplands of Kiaʻi

Honor the name of HiʻiakaikapolioPele

Mama
Memories of Sarah (Ida) Kahaulelio
Waipa Kalohapauʻole Pakele

ᔥ Eleanor Kalawaiʻakamaliʻiwahineliʻiliʻi Simeona Ahuna ᔤ

Ua hala nā kūpuna, a he ʻike kōliʻuliʻu wale nō ko kēia lā, i nā mea i ke au i hope lilo, iō kikilo. (The ancestors have passed on; today's people see but dimly times long gone and far behind.) –Mary Pukuʻi in *Place Names of Hawaiʻi* by Mary Pukuʻi, Samuel H. Elbert, and Esther T. Moʻokini.

Aunty Eleanor talks story:

Teaching Hula:

I remember Mama teaching hula.

That was in Tutu man's (Waipa) house in Keaukaha.

Long parlor: no furniture, no moena (mat), only floor—polished. Hard training for the girls: they sit with legs positioned to the side and behind them.

Mama goes to each girl. She press down on two thighs near her knees to keep the girl on the floor.

As she sways, the girl sways. As she moves in circular motion from left to right, from right to left, the girl moves. Then, she lets go of the girl's thigh so she can do it by herself—so gracefully and beautifully—

Mama taught hula to some of the prettiest girls of Keaukaha.

There were Lizzie and Lily Spalding; Lizzie Brown (I think); Tita Mano of course; Cousin Sarah, and even Aunty Edith Kanakaʻole and Gramma Mary Peʻa and Louise Kiupe Kahoilua. Aunty Edith and Gramma Mary always said "Your Mama taught us a long time ago."

Playing Slack Key Guitar:

I remember Mama and her slack key guitar music at night to lull us to sleep. And then early in the morning she would play slack key guitar again and we woke up. Such sweet music, such sweet memories, such a sweet Mama. Her music so nahenahe (soft, sweet, and melodious).

Cooking on Cracker Tin Can Stove:

I can see her early in the morning rain or shine in our small little outside cookhouse. Just a small lean-to, built right outside of and in back of our little home. She would be sitting there preparing our breakfast: tea (Spanish needles), pancakes, and whatever else she had.

I remember the little back room too that had a homemade little stove: a cracker tin can became the little stove. A portion was cut to about 2/3 way down. Then this portion was pulled down in front and carefully the sides were turned under—inside so as not to cause cuts or other accidents.
Then the can was filled with sand.
And the pot was put on 2 iron bars placed across the mid part of the can.
Cooking on this can-type-stove was very convenient.

Treating Whooping Cough:

I remember my younger sister Winona while still a little baby was sick with the whooping cough.
She was so young—just a month or so—Mama fed her sweet potato mashed very softly, feeding my sister by placing the mashed potato on the soft spot on top of her head, making motions with her mouth like she was eating.
That is how Hawaiian mothers of earlier times took care of their babies.

Mama picked and gathered some sweet potato flowers—she placed them in ti leaves and lāwalu (bound and cooked) them.
Then she took the cooked flowers, put them in to a clean white cloth and squeezed the juice on to a spoon.
She fed Sister Nona this—this lāʻau (medicine) helped my sister.

Other Medicinal Treatments:

Kaliko—ugh—that herb plant that was so plentiful then when brewed into a tea was bitter. But it was one of the best laxatives that Mama knew of.

So she had a choice—kaliko, castor oil, or " ʻūpī" (enema).

All "bad" words to us little kids way back then but—gee whiz—I don't re-member going to the doctor for any illness or having to go to the hospital.

Mama did all of that: made sure we had a clean ʻōpū (belly, stomach) and ate well, even if we had only fish and poi, or salt and poi, or palaoa mokumoku (dumpling) or palaoa lūlū (Hawaiian style mush).

And if we had fever she went looking for the pale piwa plant (all species of eucalyptus trees) to break off the little branches to use for a steam bath. And so we would hoʻopūloʻuloʻu (take a steam bath).

That was a must whenever one had a fever—if Mama could not find the pale piwa, she would use the maile honohono.

She would take the leaves of the eucalyptus of the short branches and place them in a large pot and fill with as much water as you wish and boil it.

When it boiled, she placed the pot on a padded towel on the floor and you sat by this pot filled with the hot, steaming herb water.

Mama then placed a blanket over us to cover us and keep all of the steam inside of the blanket.

This is called hoʻopūloʻuloʻu.

When you came out from under that cover—you're just wet from head to toe.

She would make sure that all the windows and doors were closed—to keep the draft out so that you will not catch the cold air because your pores were all open, having just finished with your steam bath. By this time, after you're all wiped dry and dressed again, you try rest and go to sleep.

Hoʻopūloʻuloʻu—a part of growing up.

Looking for Fish:

Mama, she knew the fishing seasons.

She was fisherman's wife.

And, she came from a fishing family.

And she knew the places to go to for certain limu (under water plants), for wana (sea urchin), for ʻopihi (limpets), for ʻaʻama (large black crab that runs over rocks on shore), for hāʻukeʻuke (a variety of sea urchin), for ʻōkole (perhaps a sea anemone).

Whenever Mama needed to prepare lunch for Dad and she had nothing at home for his lunch, she went to the beach.

When she came home she had ʻaʻama, ʻopihi, hāʻukeʻuke, some limu and she prepared his lunch.

Seems there was always poi at home.

She put his food into his lunch can and I took it to him at his working place at Pier I Kuhio Wharf (in Hilo Harbor).

Weaving Lauhala Mats:

I remember Mama weaving lauhala (pandanus leaf) mats for the floors.

All the floors had moena: the front room was the parlor and the bedroom too.

It had a 1/2" weave lauhala mat, woven wall to wall.

The middle room was Mama and Dad's bedroom and it also served as the dining room.

The sink was in this room too.

The mat in this room was 1" double weave, woven wall to wall.

And the back room had a moena woven in 1" weave, too.

Talking about wall to wall carpeting, we made them a long time ago out of lauhala. Mama wove the mats right up to the walls and fit corners also.

She would start alongside one wall, weave out about 1 foot and then she would weave back from the other end so that the weaving would be more evenly done.

When she wove out 2 or 3 feet wide, Mama would move that mat right up to the wall and then she would finish weaving—going from one side to the other. And then go back again.

She could finish a mat like this within a week, depending on the size of the room.

The moena was a very important part of our home—it provided us with warmth and beauty and it was very comfortable.

Gathering Flowers and Maile for Leis:

Mama had her kīkā (cigar flower) flower beds all around the yard.
Flowers to fashion into beautiful leis: haku lei (braided lei), kui lei (a lei stringer), maile lei, hala lei (lei made of yellow fruit sections of the Pandanus or screw pine strung together).

Roses, gardenias, gingers, ʻŌlaʻa Beauty or nani o ʻŌlaʻa (blue flower belonging to the snapdragon family), kīkā, nani aliʻi (large yellow flowers), ixora, maunaloa (the blue or white flowers of the sea bean), pua melia (plumeria), pinks, Sweet Williams, haole lehua (foreign lehua) and on and on.

Mama had lots of orders for leis. In those days you used all kinds of flowers, as much as possible.
And usually the leis had to be done within 2 days.

If the order was for maile (vine with shiny fragrant leaves), she made sure that she and Daddy or she and I went to gather the maile.

We went into the Panaʻewa forest.
First she had to find the patch.
But because it was way up in Panaʻewa, we had to catch a sampan bus.
When we found the maile patch, we gathered, or rather, she gathered and I helped.

She put them into a grass bag and she put some into a smaller grass bag for me.
If we were not going to do the leis right away, Mama put the bags with the maile inside into the bathroom to keep it cool.
When Mama would prepare and tie her maile leis, she always put them into a ti leaf pūʻolo (a bundle made out of ti leaves).
This pūʻolo kept the maile lei very nice and fresh.
And the maile is always so ʻaʻala onaona (soft, sweet smelling fragrance).

Maile hohono are beautiful flowers used in haku lei (braided lei of arranged flowers). Mama used them a lot in her lei making. Maile hohono grow untended alongside our roads, in our yards, in large fields. So beautiful, their blue so soft. When entwined into a haku lei and placed on your head, people turn and stare.

At certain times when the maunaloa flowers were in season we would wake up early in the morning and walk down to the Yacht Club Road.

There was a very large patch of maunaloa vines and when the flowers were in bloom, everybody came.
It became a fun walk to the maunaloa patch.

I remember the lovely ʻawapuhi, the yellow gingers, and the white gingers when we could find them along the Volcano Road on both sides of the road.

We would catch the bus with Mama, the whole family would go up to Panaʻewa and pick the yellow and white ginger blossoms.
We would always pick the "grass" that we used as a needle to string our ginger blossoms on the string.

A Talented Lady:
Mama was a very talented lady.
She could go to the beach early in the morning and catch enough seafood for Daddy's lunch.
She was an expert in her lauhala gathering, food preparation, slack key guitar, and raising us children.
She knew her Hawaiian medicinal herbs and took good care of us children.

I'm happy to share my mother's knowledge to help others today.
She was my best teacher.

Hale Kanaka Hou

❧ Haunani Bernardino ☙

E nā kuauli, nā kualono, nā kuamoʻo, nā kuanihi
Mai kekahi pae a i kekahi pae hou aku o Hawaiʻi mokupuni
Eia iho he hale hou, he hale kanaka, he hale wawā, he hale ola
Ua kua ʻia ke kumuuhiuhi
Ua paepae paʻa ʻia ke kahua i ka pōhaku nui me ka pōhaku liʻiliʻi
Ua kūkulu ʻia nā pou kihi me nā pou kukuna
Ua kiʻihei ʻia nā lohelau me nā pou hana
Ua ʻaho ʻia nā oʻa, ke kaupaku me ke kuaʻiole
Nā ʻaho pueo, nā ʻaho kele me nā ʻaho hui
Ua ako ʻia ka mauʻu pili me ka lauhala mai lalo aʻe a i luna o ke keʻehi
Ua ʻoki miomio ʻia a maʻemaʻe a paʻihi wale
He hale i lako i ka moena lauhala, ka hīnaʻi ʻieʻie, ka peʻahi launiu
Ka poho kukui, ka ʻumeke lāʻau a me ka ʻumeke pōhue
He hale i hoʻomākaukau ʻia ai ka iʻa, ke kalo, ka ʻuala, ka lūʻau
Ka weke a me ka ʻamaʻama
He hale i ʻoki ʻia kona piko a hāmana ka niʻo
ʻO ka hale e kū, ʻo ke kanaka e noho
He ʻōpū hālau a hewa nō, koe koena ʻole ma kūʻono
No laila e kūpipipi nā kanaka hele mai
E māhuahua aku he lau a he lau
E kipa mai nō, e komo mai a e noho mai
Ua noa ka hale kanaka hou nei
Aia hoʻi ke ola nei ē.

A New House For the People

❧ Haunani Bernardino ❧

All verdant countrysides, mountain heights, paths and trails; all mountain ridges
From one boundary end to the other boundary end of Hawai'i Island,
Behold there is a new house, a house for the people, a house of sounds, a living house.
For which was felled the uhiuhi tree,
For which was firmly laid a foundation of large stones and small stones,
For which were erected the corner posts and gable posts,
For which were lashed the wall plates and ridge posts,
For which were fitted the rafters, main ridgepole and upper ridgepole,
The main purlins, thatch purlins and support rods;
For which were thatched pili and lauhala from below to on top
And trimmed and neatly finished.
It is a house furnished with lauhala mats, 'ie'ie baskets and fans of coconut leaf,
Stone lamps, wooden calabashes and gourd calabashes,
A house for which have been prepared fish, taro, sweet potato, lū'au
Weke and 'ama'ama;
A house whose thatch over the lintel has been cut, thus opening at last its doors
to visitors.
Truly, the house that stands is the house where people shall dwell;
Of generosity the length of a long hālau though not lacking in fault, but kind and giving
With nothing hidden in recessed corners.
Let them the people step forth in great numbers,
Multiplying four hundred fold and four hundred more;
May they come, may they enter, may they dwell.
This new house for the people is open.
Indeed it lives.

Whose Nose Dat?
(A One-Act Play)

❧ Doodie Cruz ☙

Characters:

> MA: Hawaiian mother of Keala and Tita, 40 years old
>
> KEALA: Single, she is a "tita," 21 years old
>
> TITA: Glamorous, by Hawaiian standards, given name is Ku'ulei, 19 years old
>
> JIMMY: Tita's husband, clean cut young man in the military, 20 years old
>
> NURSE: (Could be male or female)
>
> TWO CHILDREN: (ages 5 and 3)

Setting:

The scene takes place in the maternity room of a hospital in Hawai'i. The room is crowded and abuzz with excitement. There are many people there bearing gifts of flowers, balloons, etc.; all are trying to get a look at "their" baby. Ma is earnestly trying to catch a glimpse of her first grandchild through the window. She is having a difficult time getting close to the window, and is visibly becoming frustrated. When she finally gets up to the window, Keala arrives and taps her on the shoulder. They both begin to search for the newest member of their family. Not long after they spot him, a nurse comes, points to the sign that says what time visiting hours are and closes the curtain. Visitors sigh then begin to leave. Fathers and immediate family members head towards the rooms, others head for the door marked EXIT. Keala and Ma are still standing in front of the window. Ma looks anxious to say something to Keala, but waits until everyone is gone.

SCENE ONE

MA: (Disappointed tone) Ai, you saw our bebe's nose?

KEALA: Wow! Whose nose dat? We no moa dat nose. Maybe Jimmy dem get…

MA: Stupid, Jimmy dem no moa dat nose, das our family's nose.

KEALA: Not! Our nose neva did look li' dat.

MA: And you know why? Cuz I wen shape you guys nose. Not easy you know for make one 'ūpepe nose cute. Yoa nose took me one year tree months, but yoa sista's nose, ho man, took me almos two yeas foa makum nice.

KEALA: Naah! I neva know dat. But how come yoa nose stay nice?

MA: My mada das why! Tutu Momi made my nose, and her mada made her nose. We all suppose to have one 'ūpepe nose, but we no moa, cuz we all wen learn how foa lomi em to makum nice.

KEALA: So what? You going fix bebe's nose or what?

MA: Not by myself. I goin show yoa sista and Jimmy how foa do um. You too! You might as well learn now and get some practice.

KEALA: Ma, I told you already, I not goin have any kids. I going buy one dog.

MA: Good! Buy one dog, buy twenty! I still goin show you how foa make, den if yoa dog get ugly nose, you can fix em.

(Both laugh)

KEALA: Ai Ma, you too much! Come on, we go see Tita.

SCENE TWO

(Women walk to daughter's room. Tita is asleep, she is lying there with full makeup on and all her Hawaiian bracelets, which go right up to her elbow. She is wearing a large hibiscus in her hair.)

KEALA: Ai Ma, look her! Full glama, she's too much! Wen you tink she had time foa put on all dat makeup? Hui, Tita! Get up, or we goin home right now.

TITA: (Weakly) Hi Mommy, hi Keala. (Whining) Ma, you saw bebe? (Ma kisses her.)

MA: Mmm. Goofy dat face.

TITA: Yah, no? You saw his nose? Ai, when Jimmy's madda sees his nose she goin…

KEALA: (Keala kisses her.) No worry, (Begins going thru Tita's goodies and gifts.) Ma goin fix em.

TITA: How you goin do dat, Ma?

KEALA: She goin show you guys how foa lomilomi his nose.

TITA: (Worried) Oh Ma…

MA: His nose not dat bad. It's just 'ūpepe. Your nose was li' dat too, like one small button. (Ma rubs the bridge of her nose.) No moa da kine, bridge.

KEALA: Bebe's button not that small, Ma.

MA: Kulikuli, Keala, or you goin get one slap. Tita, call da nurse. I like see our bebe up close.

TITA: Okay Ma. (Pushes nurse call button. Keala is still looking thru Tita's stuff.)

MA: Where's Jimmy? Did he see da bebe already?

TITA: He wen downstairs foa buy someting to eat. Ma, he's soo cute you know, see da flowas and da beah? And Ma look! He wen buy me one nada bracelet! Look what says, Aloha wau iā ʻoe e Kuʻulei. Cute yah? And look at…

(Nurse enters the room, she looks irritated.)

NURSE: Can I help you?

TITA: Yes, could you please bring my baby?

NURSE: (Sternly) Yes, but remember, you can only have two guests in here at a time.

KEALA: Yeah, yeah, we know, we wen read da sign.

(Nurse frowns, then leaves.)

I hate it wen dey treat us like we stupid or someting! Tita, can eat some of dis…?

MA: No! You go wash your hands wit soap and hot wata.

KEALA: Oh come on, Ma!

MA: Tita, you too. Go wash doze hands.

TITA: Ma, I tink we should wait till afta me and bebe go home.

MA: No, we need foa staht soon as can.

TITA: But Ma…

KEALA: Ma, Tita should stay in bed. She just had bebe dis morning.

MA: HMM, ʻkay, okay, but you go wash your hands.

KEALA: Ho man!

MA: No ho man me, Keala. Go! Now!

(Nurse rolls in bassinet with baby in it.)

NURSE: Here's your little boy, Mrs. Matthews. (She hands baby to Tita.)

TITA: Tank you!

(Nurse leaves.)

Ma, isn't he da cutest ting you eva saw? (She holds him up for them to look at.)

Who you tink he look like? Me?

KEALA: He look like bolo head Uncle Junior, 'cept foa dat nose, yeah Ma?

MA: (Fighting back her laughter.) You betta shut up, Keala. You keep making jokes li' dat and just wait till you have your own bebe. Ho, I hate to tink what he goin look like.

TITA: (Matter of factly.) One dog.

MA: What?

TITA: He goin look like one dog. (Ma and Keala look shocked.) What? Why you guys looking at me li' dat foa? (Pointing at Keala.) You da one said you not goin have kids, right? You said you goin get one dog!

(Everyone laughs.)

MA: You two goin drive me fricken crazy, I swear! Now Keala, put your sista's cookies down right now and go wash doze hands. Tita, lemme see our bebe.

(Tita gingerly hands baby to Ma.)

Ho, what a sweet face! (She holds him up to her nose and inhales deeply.) I love da smell of small babies!

(She lays him at the foot of the bed, unwraps his blanket, and begins to look him over, softly kissing each part and nodding approvingly at Tita as she completes checking it. She starts first with his ears, arms, hands (counting each finger aloud, but in a soft tone of voice), legs, feet, then the toes on the first foot, then she holds his other foot.)

One…two…three…four…five…six?

(Tita and Keala gasp, Ma starts to giggle and shakes her head.)

Nah, nah, nah, I only joking, relax.

(She kisses that foot and moves on to his chest, back, and neck. She then opens his diaper and smiles mischievously at Tita who is beaming. She rolls him over on his stomach.)

Look dis boy's bum-bum! Some nice no! (Softly stroking his bum.) Nice and round. (The three giggle.) Keala, get off yoa sista's bed and sit on dat chair.

(Ma dresses baby up again and wraps him tightly in the blanket.)

Hea, hold yoa nephew! I need foa get da baby oil from my purse. Tita, whea da hell Jimmy went foa eat?

KEALA: Maybe he wen dig out to his mada's house Mainland.

TITA: Shut up. He tol me he jus was goin downstairs.

KEALA: Ma, Ma, Ma, try look bebe's face! He stay makin funny kine!

(Ma looks over at Keala and the baby and smiles.)

MA: I tink he makin da kine.

KEALA: What kine? (Scrunches up nose, disgustedly.) Ho man! Look dis kid! He not even one day old yet and already he gonging me! Brahda, you jus wen from favorite nephew to...

MA: Gimme dat boy. And get over hea, so you learn how.

KEALA: Why I gotta learn? Whose bebe is dis? Mine?

TITA: (Giggling, then in a mock seriousness.) You heard Ma, Keala, get ova dea.

KEALA: Frick, I dunno about dis aunty ting.

(Ma changes diaper.)

MA: 'kay girls, time foa lomi dis boy's nose. I goin do um first, so watch good, okay?

Den it's yoa turn Keala. Tita, make sure you watching, cuz you da one goin do dis wen you go Mainland.

(Ma sits and cradles the baby in her arm. She puts a few drops of oil on her fingertips, then slowly and softly pinches and rubs the bridge of baby's nose. Tita and Keala watch silently in amazement. Jimmy tiptoes into the room, and is surprised to find everyone there.)

JIMMY: Oh! I didn't know you were here. I thought Ku'ulei and the baby were asleep. How are you Ma? (Kisses her on top of her head.) Hi Keala. (He kisses her on top of her head.) Hi, Honey, how are you doing? (He kisses her long and passionately.)

MA: Hui, you two! Neva mine kissing! Try watch, I stay showin you what foa do. (Both giggle.)

JIMMY: Ma, what are you doing? Is there something wrong with the baby's nose?

KEALA: Shh, she' fixin um.

JIMMY: What? Why?

TITA: 'Cuz it' 'ūpepe, Hon; you know, flat.

JIMMY: Flat? No, it's not that bad. I'm sure he'll grow out of...

MA: No, not dis nose. Dis our family's nose, you gotta lomi um foa makum nice. See, he no moa one bridge.

(Tita and Keala nod seriously in agreement. Jimmy laughs.)

JIMMY: Ma, it's really not that bad.

MA: What if lata on dis boy need foa wea glasses? Not goin stay on his face if he no moa one bridge. You lucky, Jimmy, cuz you already get (She reaches up and gingerly pinches his nose) da golden bridge.

(Everyone laughs. Ma continues to rub baby's nose.)

KEALA: Ma, wea you got dat golden bridge stuff? Tutu Momi neva say dat, ah Ma?

MA: Yoa fahda da one. He used to tease me every time. I was real da kine, serious ah, wen eva I was makin you guys nose. He every time tell everybody, No bahda her now, she stay making one golden bridge. But I tell you, every time he wen look at you guys school pictchas, he would say, Look our babies, Mommy, we made dem together, but you da one made dem beautiful.

TITA: I wish Daddy was hea Ma. I miss him.

(Keala and Ma nod silently.)

MA: He's hea baby, he always stay. (Pause) Jimmy, go wash yoa hands wit soap and hot wata. When Keala is pau, goin be yoa turn.

JIMMY: Ma, I really don't think we need to…

TITA: Jimmy, no make li' dat. You heard Ma, go wash yoa hands.

JIMMY: (Shaking his head.) Okay, Hon.

MA: Keala, go put some of da baby oil on yoa hand, jus little bit.

KEALA: 'Kay Ma. (Squeezes too much into her hand.) Oh no!

MA: I tol' you jus put little bit! You jus lomi-ing one little nose, not his whole body! Give Jimmy some of dat oil, den come sit ova hea.

(Keala changes places with Ma. Ma gives Keala the baby. She is visibly nervous.) Hold him good Keala. He not goin bite you.

KEALA: Ma, what if he staht foa cry? What if I hurt his nose?

TITA: (Giggling) You betta not hurt his nose, Keala, or I goin lick you.

KEALA: (Grumbling) Ma, Jimmy should do dis first, not me! Dis his baby!

MA: Keala, you goin wake dis boy up, den goin be moa hahd for lomi his nose. You can do it, no worry. Now softly rub his nose da way I was. (Keala begins to massage his bridge.) Yeah, yeah, yeah, jus li' dat. You doin um real good.

TITA: See Keala, you get da touch!

(Keala smiles, and continues to rub the baby's nose. She is very engrossed in what she is doing.)

KEALA: I tink wen I pau fix his nose I goin give him dimples too! Den he goin look jus like one movie stah.

MA: Heh! Tay-kit easy! We no like him get one big head, den we goin have moa foa lomilomi.

(Keala massages the baby's nose for a few minutes. During this time Jimmy is looking at the gifts, looking out the window, and watching Keala. He finally sits down next to Tita on the bed.)

TITA: Jimmy? You ready for lomi bebe's nose?

JIMMY: I don't know Ku'ulei. I'm afraid I might hurt him…

KEALA: You not. Try watch how I do um. Not dat hahd you know.

TITA: Look her, Ma, only couple minutes and she one expert already.

MA: Jimmy, you goin be alright. You and Tita need to do dis together. No can if only one person stay doin um. (Pause) Jimmy, I like you promise me…

JIMMY: What, Ma?

MA: I like you promise me dat you goin help Ku'ulei do dis. It's really important.

JIMMY: (Hesitantly) Okay, Ma, I promise.

MA: Even wen you guys move Mainland?

JIMMY: Yes, even after we move to the Mainland.

MA: Good! I always tol everybody dat you were one good boy, Jimmy, even dough you no moa Hawaiian blood. (She reaches out and touches his chest.) Yoa heart stay Hawaiian. You always do tings da Hawaiian way. Somebody only need foa show you how one time, das all. My Tita's lucky she found you. (Reaching over and touching the baby.) Dis boy get one good fahda. (Ma kisses Jimmy.) You get one nada brahda or what for dis hahd head Keala who only like dogs?

JIMMY: Sorry, Ma, I'm the only son. But maybe I could introduce Keala to my…

KEALA: No act! I no need you foa help me find one boyfriend. Now get ova hea and make dis boy's nose.

(Keala hands the baby to Jimmy and trades places with him. Ma coaches Jimmy softly. Tita and Keala watch with pride. No one notices the nurse entering.)

NURSE: Excuse me, but the rules clearly state that there can be only two visitors at a time in the patient's room. I need to ask one of you to wait outside.

KEALA: Why? We not boddering anybody. We not making big noise. Our mahda stay showing us how foa lomi da baby's nose.

NURSE: I'm sorry, but the rules clearly state that…

KEALA: What's da big deal?

JIMMY: (Rises, and is about to hand the baby to Tita.) I'll wait outside.

KEALA: Oh no! You not getting off dat easy brahda. You sit down, I goin wait outside. (She kisses Tita, then says to the nurse) Come on, Miss Rules, (as she walks out the door) can only have two visitors at a time in da room, read da sign, close da curten wen everybody still dea, neva smile at nobody...

(Jimmy sits back down and continues to massage the baby's nose. The nurse and Keala are gone. Tita notices Ma is looking out the window, lost in thought.)

TITA: Ma? (She does not respond.) Mommy? (She still does not answer Tita.) Jimmy, give me da baby and check Ma, please. Someting must be boddering her. I hope she not sick.

(Jimmy walks over to Ma, and puts his arm around her.)

JIMMY: (Softly) Ma? Are you okay? Can I get you something? Maybe you should sit.

(She shakes her head, and gently pushes him away.)

MA: Wen you guys goin Mainland?

JIMMY: Well...I'm going to leave in two months, then I'll send for Ku'ulei and the baby as soon as I find us a place to live. I applied for base housing, but if it doesn't come through, I'll have to find something else. Maybe outside the base. I hope it doesn't take more than a month.

MA: So tree months?

JIMMY: Yes, if we're lucky, about three months altogether.

MA: Das so soon. We goin have to really work hahd on da baby's nose. Make sure dat everytime somebody hold da boy, dey lomi his nose. Tita, wen you lomi baby's nose you should always use baby oil or lotion. If no moa den da Wesson oil is okay. But only need little bit. No put planty. You only massaging his nose, not frying akule.

TITA: No worry Ma, we goin do um jus like you, yah no, Jimmy?

JIMMY: Sure! But I don't know about the Wesson oil. (Pause) Ma, how many minutes a day should we do this?

MA: As much as can.

(Keala enters the room, laughing to herself.)

TITA: What you laughing about, mento?

KEALA: Dat nurse! She sooo da kine...busy. Her was outside tryin foa watch every single room on dis floor! Soon as she see da tird person go inside da room, quick she run ova dea chase dem out. I was making da kine to her... I make like I goin come in, den she run ova by me, den I make like I not goin come in. Now she all haboot[1] at me. She tol me (Imitating the nurse.) I think you should leave. I tol her I tink you should jus worry about being one nurse not one security gahd. Anyway... I goin, bum bye dey trow Tita dem out early, den I goin have to watch dis small boy at home. (She kisses everyone goodbye.)

MA: Keala, cook two cup rice wen you get home, okay?

KEALA: 'Kay Ma, a hui hou!

MA: You know what, try wait, I goin wit you.

JIMMY: Ma, you don't have to leave.

TITA: Yah, Ma, no go, stay wit us.

MA: No, I goin home cook dinna. Jimmy, no eat da food downstairs, not dat 'ono, and too expensive. I goin make you one big plate. What you like drink?

JIMMY: Mmm, how about a Coke?

MA: Okay, I see you guys lata. Don't forget dat baby's nose.

TITA/JIMMY: Okay Ma.

(She kisses both of them, then they leave.)

SCENE THREE

(Scene takes place in the home of Jimmy and Tita a few years later. It is somewhat chaotic. You can see the living room and the dining room at the same time. Tita is sitting at the dining room table trying to write a letter. Jimmy chases their noisy children around the room. A football game is on television.)

JIMMY: Come on! The game's about to start. Our favorite team is playing. (Begins chanting.) Go Boys go! Go Boys go! Go Boys go! (Children join in with the chanting as they continue to run around.) Ku'ulei! Can you please help me? The game's about to start.

TITA: Jimmy, I'm trying to write this letter to Ma them. You two! Sit down now!

(Ikaika, the oldest one, sits down immediately on the couch. The youngest one, Kaena, continues to run around and chant. Tita shakes her head and goes after Kaena. Jimmy stops chasing him and sits down next to Ikaika. Both are glued to

---

[1] Haboot: local slang for angry

the television. Tita catches Kaena and plops him down next to his father. She heads back to the diningroom table and begins writing again. Without taking his attention away from the television, Jimmy taps his leg and Kaena automatically lays his head on his father's lap. He taps Ikaika's leg.)

JIMMY: Go get the baby oil.

(While waiting, he gently strokes Kaena's head. Ikaika exits the stage, then returns with the oil to the couch. Jimmy is talking to the television, behaving like the classic armchair quarterback. Ikaika hands father the oil and hops back on the couch next to him. Jimmy opens the bottle and puts two drops on his fingertips, then closes and places the bottle on the floor. He softly and slowly begins to massage Kaena's nose, the whole while still yelling at the television. Tita is talking to herself at the table.)

TITA: Dear Ma and Keala...no, Aloha Ma and Keala... no, Dearest Ma and Keala...(sighs) I hate to write letters. Honey, I'm going to call Ma them. Can you turn the tv down, please? Just a little.

JIMMY: Sure! Honey, can you bring me a beer before you call?

TITA: (Sighs) Can't you get it?

JIMMY: Come on! I'm lomi-ing Kaena's nose.

TITA: Okay, okay.

(She gets and gives him a beer and hands a snack to Ikaika. Then Kaena starts to fidget. She hands him a snack also.)

Don't eat this lying down. Okay? When Daddy is through lomi-ing your nose, then you can eat this. Understand?

(Kaena nods. Tita goes back to the dining room, dials the phone, and waits for someone to answer.)

Ma? Hi, it's me!... Oh stop it, Ma, you know who this is. How are you folks doing?... Oh that's great... They're fine... Yeah, getting really big... Uh huh... No, they're not asleep... Right now they're watching football with their father... Yes... So is Keala there?... Tell her to pick up the other phone... (Laughs) Not! Hey Jimmy, Ma said I sound like a real Haole. Howzit Keala?... Did you folks get the pictures?... Don't their noses look perfect?... Sure, everyday. As a matter of fact, Jimmy is doing Kaena's nose now... Uh huh... Even Ikaika helps... (Laughs) Yeah, yeah, I know. Thank you, Ma, you too, Keala...

For Grampa and Gramma and Summers, With Love

❧ J.W. MAKANUI ❧

Makaweli red dirt
goin stain your slippas
no matter how hard you scrub
and going be shame
when you gotta go back school
cause your feet
going look all lepo

Makaweli red dirt
going stain your face
cause you was eating
sticky, drippy mango,
or lychee,
or, mo' worse,
cause you get
hanabata

Makaweli red dirt
going stain all your clothes
no matter how hard you try
for stay clean
and Gramma going snap
cause gotta wash clothes
every day you stay visit

BUT
Makaweli red dirt
going get in your body
and put one stain on your heart

that going stay till you die
and the stain
going keep calling you back
calling and comforting
with memories
and moments
of summers
with love.

Daddy Wen *Make* But He Still Wen Tell Me Something

❧ MURIEL MILILANI AH SING HUGHES ☙

My Aunty Helen wen tell me I was special because my fada wen talk to me… from the grave. Maybe as why he named me Mililani or Heaven's pet. I don't know. I never feel special. I just wen get one dream.

My dad was 53 when I was born. He was one old buggah. All my friends had young parents. I was stuck with parents who was some old. More worse, as long as I can remember, my dad walked with one cane and dragged his mumu left foot behind him. He wen get one stroke when I was two years old. I remember the tunk… tunk of his cane as he walked down our long hallway. So we never went camping or hiking or fishing like the other kids. He never like go to the movie theater because he was scared might have one fire and he no can get out. He never work already so I used to spend plenty time with him, talking story and just hanging out. I wen even listen to his favorite Red Sox baseball games on the radio on those hot Lahaina afternoons. He used to tell me about his young days on Moloka'i. Dad told me about the red shark, our 'aumakua, and how this guardian spirit protect us if we have trouble in the ocean. Hanging out with Dad meant I never had to do my chores.

The summer of my eighth grade year, Dad got really sick. Dr. Peterson told my mada for call all the family. They do that when the patient ready for make. My brothers and sisters came home to Lahaina and waited for Dad to die. But he never. So everyone went back home. That summer, I wen decide I going write the stories Dad wen tell. I was going to write the name of the red shark in case I got lost at sea. Yep, I was going to do these things. Guarans, ball-bearin's.

But I never. Time wen fly by and Dad got sick again the next year. They wen call all the family again. Same like last year. But this time, Dad wen fool us all… he was really dying. Was one Sunday night. Dad had real hard time breathing. His lips was some dry so I wen use the straw for put some water to wet his lips. He was making big noise, calling for Ma. I was trying for tell him to be quiet. I never like him make ass, as why. But he kept on calling. His breathing was like rattling in one empty package. And he had one strange smell, too. Was one kinda sweet but musty smell. I never know as was the smell of death. I told my mada that I like stay over at the hospital. But she told me no act silly. I had to go back to Lahaina because had school on Monday. She never like listen to me so I had to go home with my cousins.

Monday morning, my cousin Sherl came looking for me at the band room. She said I had to go with her because my dad was dying. She went to Kuhua Camp to look for her aunty to baby-sit her kid. But never get anybody at the house. Finally, we went to Sherl's house and saw the aunty waiting there. We left the baby and rushed to the Wailuku hospital. When we got there, my mada was crying. "I told Daddy to wait. I told him you was coming," mom sobbed. I was thinking, what can one 13-year-old kid do for one dying man? My cousin Sherl wen break down and cry. Her husband Kazu wen hug her and just let her sob her heart out. I think she was sad because I never saw my dad die. I never like tell anybody but I never like see him die. As too much for one young kid like me.

All the finally came over to our house. My Chinese aunties came from Honolulu with their powdered faces, pearl earrings, and jade rings. My Hawaiian aunties came from Kalihi with their hugs, kisses, food and music. Our poi dog house was full of all kind people. I had to sleep in my fada's room because everybody was too scared. My sister Rose's baby just cry in Dad's room but not me, I no scared.

The night before the funeral, I dreamed I saw my dad. He never talk to me, though. Just like he had one narrator. I remember hearing my Chinese aunties moaning about the fact that we were going to cremate my dad and scatter his ashes outside of Lahaina harbor. "Our brother, Ah Nee, going be floating in the ocean for eternity," Aunty Helen said, trying to convince my mada to change her mind. Then the dream narrator wen tell me not to forget my dad's cane. Dad didn't have his cane for his Chinese eternity.

When I woke up, the family was in the kitchen eating breakfast. I wen ask my mada where Dad's cane was. She told me was right behind the kitchen door. I told her about my dream. So my mada wen put the cane into my dad's coffin. She wen tell my Chinese aunties because when we went to the boat harbor, my aunties were crying and telling me how lucky I was that my dad talked to me. My Chinese aunties never like get on the boat with us. I can see them standing on the dock and talking how Ah Nee talked to me. Only thing is he never talk to me. His dream narrator wen talk for him. Maybe someday, Dad going talk to me himself. Until then, I no scared. I just gotta wait. Someday, I going be special enough for my dad to talk to me.

Purple Fingers

❧ N. Keonaona Aea ❧

Sunday afternoon, when church is pau, we go to the 7-11 just off the 405 Freeway. Lou and I buy Slurpees for the kids. We tell them to pretend it's shave ice—not snow cones, because there's a big difference. We haven't been to Hawai'i for about five years now, so the kids don't remember anything about shave ice. It costs full airfare for all of us to fly, but my husband and I are saving our money for a house. Sometimes I don't know if that's smart. The kids don't have a lot of nice things because the extra money goes into our House Account. By the time we buy a home, nobody will be living with us—the kids will be grown and gone. That's how I feel sometimes.

I like Sundays. We go to church in our blue Subaru station wagon, then come home for a big brunch. Sonny is getting older (he's 13) and says he doesn't like Sunday school because it's babyish. But Ululani is different: she's eleven and still likes church, her stuffed animals, cartoons, even being with her brother. She's also very pretty, and very unaware of how pretty she is. Boys are starting to call her on the phone which bothers Lou and me a lot.

He puts them on the speakerphone. "You have one minute to talk to my daughter. Her mother and I are right here listening to every word." Ululani thinks everything in life is funny. She giggles when we hear the dial tone.

Last week someone named Rexton called. "You're on a speakerphone," Lou barked.

"That's okay. Hey, Ululani, you want to come ice skating with me and my family?" Rexton asked.

"No. She cannot go any place with you," Lou said.

"Not to that place in Culver City? Right up the street?" Rexton asked. He sounded like he'd been told he couldn't go to the corner store for soda.

"Sorry. My husband and I don't know you," I said.

"—or your family," Lou butted in. "Good-bye."

Two minutes later the phone rang. "This is Rexton. Can we meet you? My folks say tomorrow's a good time…you want to talk to them first?"

Lou and I stared at each other. It dawned on us that we were hearing the voice of a young black boy. Ululani grinned. I motioned Lou to be quiet and said, "No, that's okay, Rexton. We'll speak with them, and you, tomorrow."

"Okay. What time?"

"How about six-thirty, dinner time!" Ululani shouted. I pretended to choke her while Lou shook his head frantically.

We heard muffled words of surprise before Rexton said, "My folks says all right and thank you. See you tomorrow, Ulu."

I scolded her and said she had no right making plans without asking me or her father first. Besides, what was I supposed to fix for dinner? "I mean, what do those people eat?" I fumed.

"He likes Dr. Pepper and nachos, but not Slurpees," my daughter said.

That night I actually thought about Slurpees, then shave ice, then Hawai'i, then myself at Ululani's age eating lunch at Grandma's on Sunday afternoons. Me and my cousins, uncles, and aunties sitting around one big table at the Kaimuki house. Before I fell asleep, I knew what I'd be cooking the next day.

I didn't go to church. Even Sonny stayed home because I needed help with the food. First we went to two restaurants and three grocery stores in Gardena. Almost everything I bought had to be refrigerated, except for the big leaves wrapped in newspaper. I poured it into a pile on the kitchen floor and sat cross-legged before it.

"Do like me," I said to my son. I picked up a large, smooth leaf. "Get a knife and cut off the stem. Then you hold the leaf here and strip off the hard part of the rib, see?" I cut the stem, then peeled off the hard membrane.

"Got it," said Sonny.

We cut and stripped the five pounds of taro leaves. When we were pau our fingers were stained purple. I rinsed the leaves in the sink and dropped them in a big pot while Sonny opened a can of coconut milk.

Then I cubed three pounds of chicken. Sonny started the rice. I emptied the bag of thick poi into a bowl and added water. Then I mixed it by hand while Sonny cut the manapua in half and laid them on a plate. We nibbled at the red pork and crumbs from the sweet dough. I found an easy haupia recipe (Combine coconut milk, cornstarch, sugar, and water in double boiler. Pour into pan. Refrigerate). Sonny carefully measured and stirred the ingredients; I sliced a pineapple, then rubbed it lightly with salt to bring out the sweetness. We took turns stirring the chicken lū'au.

Everything smelled 'ono. I forgot about Ululani and the brave boy we'd be meeting in a few hours. I forgot about our cramped apartment and the bigger house we hoped to buy. That afternoon in my kitchen, I forgot about L.A.

Rexton and his parents were twenty minutes late, which worked out well. I'd sent Lou to the store for rainbow sherbert and they all arrived at the front door at about the same time. The Carter's were big, dark people—especially Mr. Carter. His eyes and teeth looked super white. We shook hands on the porch while Ululani half jokingly told Rexton to take off his shoes. "My mom will pull your ears if you wear those dirty things in here," she said. I scowled at her while Rexton hastily untied his Nikes.

Then Mrs. Carter shyly, almost apologetically, gave me something wrapped in paper. She said it was the only thing that grew well outside their apartment and hoped I would like them as much as she did. I cradled the bundle in one arm and unwrapped five brilliant Bird-of-Paradise flowers.

"These are perfect," I said. For truly, they were.

While I poured drinks, Lou served the food. "This is poi," he announced. He set small, individual servings on the table. "Most people think it tastes good with sugar. But not us. If you eat it with lū'au or something salty, it tastes really 'ono together. See? Look…" He uncovered the steaming pot of thick, dark leaves and stirred it slowly. "…this is the leaf part of the taro plant. Poi is the bottom part of the same plant."

Our guests stared at the gray poi, dark green lū'au, bits of red pork spilling from the manapua, the bowl of fluffy white rice and the jiggly cubes of haupia. When Mr. And Mrs. Carter glanced tentatively at their plates, I was glad we weren't serving laulau and 'opihi.

"Well, let's eat. If this doesn't fill us we can always redeem those Taco Bell coupons, " I said nervously. I began to wish I'd listened to Ululani about buying nachos. After all, this little gathering was in her honor—not that she seemed to remember or care. I stared hard at her, hoping she'd read my look. Chew with your mouth closed and use your napkin. But she was too busy clinking her juice glass against Sonny's ("Banzai!") and coaxing Rexton to follow.

I thought I'd eat with the serious pleasure I did during Hawaiian family gatherings. Here, before us, was the food that tied us to our culture. Yet something began nagging at me when I'd been given those beautiful, hand-picked flowers. I grew aware in my gut, my na'au, that I'd misjudged and disrespected this occasion:

I had planned tonight's menu to test our guests. If they could not appreciate these unusual dishes, then they could not include Ululani in their wholesome family outings. I was reserving the right to personalize their acceptance or rejection of my Hawaiian food. What would Grandma say if she knew I'd mixed the poi, cleaned the lūʻau, cut the fruit and even set the table with this kind of attitude?

As Lou mumbled a simple dinner grace, I glanced at the bowed heads, the tight black hair and strong necks of my daughter's friends. I studied their folded hands, then mine—stained purple, but not as completely dark or rich as theirs.

In my shame, I said my own silent prayer.

We ate. Our guests began with polite nibbles and neutral expressions, then became more animated as they discovered something genuinely tasty, something to request as second helpings. For Rexton it was the haupia and manapua. For Mr. Carter it was the poi—with sugar, and the chicken lūʻau. ("Mmm…finer than greens. You ever had greens with pork bones? How you all fix pork, anyway?") Mrs. Carter liked the manapua, lūʻau, and pineapple. As she wiped juice from her chin with her hand, she said, "Shouldn't waste something so delicious on a napkin." Then she calmly licked her fingers Kentucky-Fried-Chicken-style while Ululani grinned at her, then me. I noticed, too, that when Mr. Carter laughed (which was often) he didn't cover his cavernous mouth.

We learned that Rexton was twelve, didn't like basketball, but was a good swimmer. "And I never ice skated. So if you all let Ulu come to the Culver City rink, then I'll look good since she's a girl, and girls are worse learners than guys!" He glanced at Ululani who looked at her father, but he was too busy talking to Mr. Carter about pukas in the ground, wet burlap bags and heated rocks. When Mr. Carter tried to pronounce kalua pig (Carlew Ping?), they laughed. Two men with their mouths open and full of Hawaiian food. I pulled my plate close, set my elbows on the table and dug in, just like I did when I was a kid surrounded by ʻohana.

So it was decided. Before the last bite of sherbert had been swallowed, before the final drop of coffee poured, before our ʻōpūʻs were given a final satisfying rub—we knew our kids would do well as friends. And so would we, their parents. I was grateful that this dinner, begun with misguided pride and intentions, had been graciously used to turn this into an evening we'd all remember.

Grandma would have been pleased.

Dreamtime from the Fisherman's Woman

⚶ NALANIKANAKA'OLE ⚶

where is the pond of the fisherman's woman
near the spring clearing at fragrant hala blooming
she is there to soak in leaves of thought
with hairstrands long like black seaweed
flowing supple at the seagate
submerged white hala bundles catch light
    tied
    strung
    and left weighted
till a more pliable moment

the morning stirs in long plaiting weaves
crossing calm seas the porpoises return
    return from the bay where the yellow waters run
    return from dark waters flowing
    return from fragrant hala blooming
    return to the bay of the skilled fisherman
they circle at the point of placed offering altar
in swift pursuit where the winds change
staggered arches tack out into the blue
taking heed of the ominous
the skilled fisherman prepares to wander
    tying taut the sails
    tugging at the rigs
    wetting down the lashings
firming the hold of the fishing gourd
a silent offering
in launching gait
a run on board

held in balance
the bow cuts into the trades

by forties they soar
to the heights of the wrasse
    roosting high in the cavetops
    gliding seaward to bathe in the mist
    diving seaward to feed in the frenzy
by forties they soar
where the dog eyes the heavens
wedged into formation
in the shelter of the bay
by forties they soar
to wheel at the shining
hovering slow over the sand banks
in windless silence
by forties they soar

NOTE: for additional information and some insights on the author and the work, see the interview by Chanda Hina Curtice on page 116.

Mōhala Ka Pua: The Flower Blooms

❧ PUALANI KANAKAʻOLE KANAHELE ❧

The silence of early morning was broken with the cry of a newborn baby. The light of morning streamed through the window of Waiolama's house. She had just given birth to a baby girl. Waiolama or Lama, as she was affectionately known to her family, and her husband Haʻaloʻu had just had their hiapo (their first born child). Haʻaloʻu had wanted a boy; however, they were both happy to have a healthy baby, for they had waited eight years before Lama finally became pregnant. Now the baby's cry announced the reality of the beginning of their family. This was an exciting occasion, a time for celebration.

ʻŌlena, the older sister of Lama, was the pale-keiki (the mid-wife) who delivered the newborn. ʻŌlena was trained by her father's mother in the profession of lāʻau lapaʻau (the medicinal and herbal healer). She delivered her nephews, nieces, cousins, and cared for the rest of the family during their ailments.

After this delivery, ʻŌlena went outside to enjoy the early light of the sun and the cool breeze. She reflected upon the simultaneous appearance of the sun streaming through the window and the head of the baby in her hands. "He hōʻailona (a sign or omen)!" she thought. Her lāʻau lapaʻau practice provided these auspicious moments and she thanked those who gave her this knowledge of healing.

ʻŌlena walked back into the house and asked Lama, "Did you two pick a name yet?"

"No, Haʻaloʻu had some ideas and so did I but we couldn't decide so we waited to see if anything significant would happen and it hasn't," said Lama.

"Well, I'm sure a proper name will surface," replied ʻŌlena as she thought of her hōʻailona. "I'm leaving, I'll stop at Mama's and give her the good news." ʻŌlena leaned over to kiss her sister and the baby. With a smile she whispered to Lama, "Pupuka kēia keiki,"[1] you'll have a hard time keeping up with her, Lama. I'll prepare dinner for you two this evening, hui hou, see you again."

---

[1] Literally "this child is ugly," but this phrase is used to offset the intention of expressing admiration as a means of protection for the child.

Lama called after her sister not to cook; however, before she could finish, she heard, "Hū-i, hū-i, e Lama!"[2] and ʻŌlena came back in the house with their mother.

Lama answered, "Aloha kakahiaka, e Māmā!"[3]

Their mother, Kaipalaoa, was very serious this morning. Before the sisters said another word, their mother asked, "How is the baby? Is she healthy?"

"She's fine but how did you know it was a girl?" questioned ʻŌlena.

Kaipalaoa signaled ʻŌlena to go and sit on the bed with her sister. Kaipalaoa, or Kai as she was sometimes called, kissed Lama, took the baby and sat in the rocking chair. She inspected the shape of the baby's head and nodded her approval. She touched the manawa (the fontanel) very gently to see if it was open. " ʻŌ, maikaʻi (good)!" she whispered. As her fingers moved to the forehead, she said, "He lae puʻu, he akamai ʻo ia."[4] Kai unwrapped the blanket to inspect the arms, fingers, legs and toes. She pulled, stretched, and measured them. Kai smiled and rewrapped the baby.

ʻŌlena and Lama had seen their mother inspect all her grandchildren in the very same way; however, this seemed so much more intense than before. ʻŌlena asked, "What are you looking for, Mama?"

Kai murmured, "Inspecting the bundle from our ancestors. First the head is inspected. It is the most important spot; if the head is round without flat spots, it is perfect. It is a good place for the ʻaumakua (ancestral guardian) to come and visit. If the head is flat or crooked, then it has to be shaped. The high forehead with a little puʻu (protuberance) is a sign that the child is smart. The pepeiao (ears) must be close to the side of the poʻo (head). The nose should not sit on the face but must be pulled and shaped." Kai stopped for a moment and stared at the baby, then put her down.

"He aha ka pilikia, e Māmā?"[5] asked ʻŌlena.

Kai did not answer the question but turned to Lama and asked, "I hea lā ʻo Haʻaloʻu, kāu kāne, e Lama? E kāhea iā ia."[6] Lama recognized the urgency in

---

[2] "Haloo, haloo, Lama!"
[3] "Good morning, Mama!"
[4] "A protruding forehead, she is a smart one."
[5] "What's the problem, Mama?"
[6] "Where is Haʻaloʻu, your husband, Lama? Call him."

her mother's face and called her husband. Haʻaloʻu walked into the room and was surprised to see Kai. He started to walk over to kiss her; however, with a flick of her wrist she signaled him to sit next to his wife.

Kaipalaoa began to reveal her reason for coming over early this morning. "I had a dream last night and another this morning. I was young in the first dream. It was during the early years of my marriage to your father. My mother came to the house and put her hands on my ʻōpū (stomach) and said, 'be patient, our baby will arrive soon.' She smiled and I woke up. It startled me to see my mother and feel her like she was actually in the room with me. I couldn't go back to sleep for awhile; however, when I finally fell asleep again, I had another dream.

"My mother was also in the second dream. This time she was older, much as the way she looked before she died. She was wearing her favorite pāʻū (dance skirt) and a lei liko lehua (a neck wreath) of young lehua leaves. I watched her dance and her movements were so swift that when she brushed by me doing the welina (a particular foot movement) I could smell the fragrance of her kappa (tapa) and it reminded me of my childhood and the Luhaupua wind (a pleasant wind associated with dew and flowers) of ʻŌlaʻa. When the Luhaupua blew, the fragrance of the forest came with it."

Kai stopped for a moment, obviously excited by her revealing dream, then she continued, this time speaking in Hawaiian:

"A kū ʻo ia i koʻu alo, alaila nō, ua minoaka a ʻōlelo iaʻu, 'Ia nō ʻo ia, kā kāua hoa, ka hoa pili me nā kūpuna.'

"She stopped before me, then smiled and said to me, 'She's here, our companion, the link to the ancestors.'

" 'Hoʻokuʻi i ka lani, hoʻokuʻi i ka pae ʻāina mai Hāʻena a Hāʻena. 'O ia nō ka lā naue i ka lani,' alaila nō ua ala au."

" 'Joining the heavens, joining the earth, joining the islands from Hāʻena to Hāʻena. She is the sun which moves in the heavens,' then I woke up."

Kai paused and then continued, "When I woke up, it seemed like there was someone standing by me and shaking me. I glanced around the room and there was no one there. I got out of bed, changed my clothes and went to the lānai. I sat in the dark, in the cool morning, thinking about the dreams and my mother. I remembered my mother's words exactly the way I just told you. I didn't understand the dream and it bothered me. I looked toward the ocean and thought, 'Mālie ke kai a ka hālāwai.'[7] My eyes searched the horizon as ua puka a'ela ka hā'ena a ka lā mai ka moana.[8] When I saw that first breath of the sun, I understood my dream. I knew a baby was being born. Then I thought of you, Waiolama. I started walking over here and as I walked, I knew the baby was here and it was a girl. She will be the one I teach our oli (chant) and hula. Lama, she is the bridge from our kūpuna (elders or ancestors)."

'Ōlena burst out, "Oh, Mama, I have chicken skin! It was at that time, at the first light, that I helped the baby out; she cried out before the pa'i (slap)."

Kaipalaoa looked at her daughter and son-in-law and said, "I want to take this baby and raise her with the help of our kūpuna. All the things I was taught, I want to teach her. She will be the link from the past to the future."

When Kai finished, there was silence. Everyone in the room stared at the floor except Kai who looked intently at Lama and Ha'alo'u. She sensed rejection but waited for their verbal reaction. This choice was between Kaipalaoa's family tradition and Waiolama's desire to be a mother.

The new parents looked at each other, then Ha'alo'u took his wife's hand and softly said, "She is your mother, whatever you decide, I will support."

The silence was broken by Lama's wailing for her baby; however, no one said anything or tried to comfort her. After a few minutes of crying Lama calmed down, wiped her eyes and composed herself. With her eyes focusing on her hands she attempted to answer her mother:

"E ku'u Māmā, nui ko'u aloha nou, 'o ko'u Māmā 'oe. Ua hānai a mālama 'oe ia'u, 'a'ole i mālama kou Māmā ia'u. 'O kou kuleana ia. A i ia manawa 'oe ia'u, 'a'ole i mālama i ku'u pēpē. He 'ano luahine 'oe i ia manawa. Pono 'oe e hui pū me kou mau hoaaloha."

"My mother, my love for you is great, you are my mother. You fed and took care of me; it wasn't your mother who took care of me. It was your responsibility. And now I will take care of my baby. You are older now. You should get together with your friends."

---

[7] 'The sea was calm, all the way to the horizon.'
[8] "The intense breath of the sun emerged from the ocean."

"Tshā!" Kai said:

"Pala naio a holo pūpule nō lākou. He mea nui kēia hana, no nā kūpuna a mākua a kamali'i a mo'opuna a pēlā nō. 'O ia ku'u 'ī wale iā 'olua. E ho'i ana au!"

"They run around and don't do anything worthwhile. This is an important task from the grandparents to our parents to the children and grandchildren. This is all I'm going to say to you. I'm going home."

Kai walked quickly out to the front gate. Then, with the gate in hand, she paused and turned around. 'Ōlena was happy to see her mother returning and hoped that this birth would be celebrated.

Kai made two demands: "Waiolama, the name for the child is Kalānaueikalani and I don't want this incident mentioned ever again!" She turned and walked away.

Ha'alo'u came in quietly to comfort his wife. He picked up the baby and gave her to Lama. She looked at the baby sadly and whispered, "'O Kalānaueikalani kou inoa, e ku'u hiwahiwa."[9]

Many years later—

"Kalānaueikalani, Kalānaue, Naue, where are you?"

"I'm in the kitchen eating breakfast, Mama!" answered the girl.

"When you're finished, go to grandma's house, gather her laundry and bring it back. I want to wash today, it's a nice day to hang the clothes out to dry." A heavy sigh is heard by Lama, then silence. "Naue, did you hear me? Where is that girl?" she mumbled.

"I heard you, Mama," she said as she walked on to the lanai where her mother was working. "What are you doing?"

"Kuiki kapa (quilting). Why are you frowning?"

"Well," said Kalānaue, "I don't like to go to grandma's house. I don't think she likes me. She hardly ever says anything to me and she's so grouchy."

"Tshā, don't talk like that, silly girl, of course your grandmother loves you. Now go get her laundry so I can do it this morning."

---

[9] "Kalānaueikalani is your name, my precious one."

"Okay, I will, Mama. I'll see you soon," shouted Naue as she walked slowly down the trail which led to her grandma's house.

Lama watched her daughter shuffle off towards her mother's house. Her thoughts were on Kalānaue's comments about her grandmother, Kai. Lama still felt guilty about her mother's disappointment at the birth of Kalānaue fourteen years before. That unhappy incident had not been mentioned since.

Kaipalaoa was a well known teacher of Haʻa, a dance style she learned during her childhood from her Tūtū Makuʻu, who was an older brother of her mother, Puʻuone. Kaipalaoa was raised in Hula Kapu[10] by her Tūtū Makuʻu.

In his generation Makuʻu was given the privilege as this family's tradition bearer. Puʻuone was his star dancer; however, Makuʻu chose Kaipalaoa, at her birth, to carry on this tradition. Now she had the responsibility to maintain and find another in her family to continue this practice.

As Kalānaue approached her grandmother's house she was totally surprised at what she heard. She didn't recall hearing her grandmother chant before. She knew that Kai went to visit her aging uncle, Makakupu, who lived in Kaʻū. Naue thought perhaps her grandmother learned this new found talent in Kaʻū. Kai was out on the back lānai chanting. Since she didn't want to disturb her, Kalānaue decided to gather the laundry and take it home without asking her grandmother. She went from room to room picking up towels, linen and clothing. As she entered the bedroom, she noticed an old trunk which had been utilized as a television stand for a long time. It was standing open. Out of curiosity she peeked in and to her delight saw some old books, an old ʻulīʻulī (a gourd rattle with feathers on top used to keep the rhythm while dancing), a quilt, and other things she didn't recognize.

She listened for her grandmother but Kai continued to chant. Kalānaue quickly grabbed the book on the very top and opened it. Her heart beat rapidly as she turned to the first page. There was a note written in fancy, old handwriting and she read:

To My Moʻopuna (grandchild),
I wanted to leave you something of great value which belongs to our

---

[10] Hula Kapu: A very rigid style of teaching hula and passing on the family tradition from one generation to the next. This teaching style incorporates the dedication of the bearer to the Gods. Hula Kapu literally means dance and dancer are sacred to the Gods.

family. I wanted to teach you these mele hula, dance chants, mele oli (songs to chant), and mele pule (prayer chants or prayer songs); however, this was not to be. I've written all I know, and hope some day, maybe…

As Kalānaue glanced through the book, she found page after page of chants written in fancy old handwriting. Chants to Hiʻiaka, to Laka, to Haʻiwahine, to Pele, to Popoki, and many others. These names were not familiar to her but it was exciting to discover this. She listened again for her grandmother but this time there was silence. Kai had stopped chanting. Thinking her grandmother might come in, Naue closed the book quickly and returned it to the trunk. She picked up her laundry bundle and was ready to leave when she heard voices outside. "I wonder who Grandma is talking to? I don't know that voice," she thought. As she walked down the stairs, the beating of the ipu (a gourd instrument) began.

Everything was strange, the chanting, the opened trunk, the book, the stranger Grandma was talking to, the instrument she was beating. She reviewed all this in her mind and promptly forgot about it until the next morning.

"E Kalānaue, ua ala ʻoe, Kalānaue?[11] I'm going holoholo, gather sea food or go fishing; you come with me. Hurry, wake up and bring the ʻohua (baby manini or reef surgeon fish) net in the corner. Hurry, the tide is low," shouted Lama. When she heard ʻohua net, Kalānaue stumbled out of bed and hurried to get ready. Only in late May or June they went fishing for ʻohua and she really enjoyed catching and eating them.

When they arrived at the beach, the ocean was calm. The tide had just gone out, leaving the area dotted with tide pools and the smell of seaweed. Lama didn't say a word but placed the net immediately in the shallow tide pools. She pushed the net under the rocks and shook it, then placed it between the cracks and shook it again, then she pulled it up and there were the ʻohua jumping and squirming in the net. Lama put the ʻohua in the bag tied to her waist. Then she handed the net to Kalānaue.

"Remember," said Lama, "stay in the small ponds. If you go into the deep water, they can get away easily. Push them into a corner. If they can't swim, they can't

11 "Kalānaue, are you up?"

get away." Kalānaue had a great time and also caught some fish. "Well, I think this is enough for now. What do you think, Kalānaue? Shall we go home?" Lama said.

"Yes, we have enough. Let's go home, Mama. Are we going to dry these or eat them raw?"

"We'll do both and give some to Grandma."

Thoughts of the previous day rushed back to Kalānaue and she asked her mother. "Mama, I heard Grandma chanting yesterday when I went to fetch her laundry; was she teaching someone?"

Lama was surprised to hear this and she questioned her daughter, "Are you sure she was chanting? Maybe she was singing?"

"No! She was chanting like you do sometimes. She was chanting for a long time, then she stopped and talked to someone. I didn't recognize the voice. I didn't bother her and she didn't know I was there. As I was leaving, I heard her beating the ipu."

Lama was confused at her mother's renewed interest in the hula and chant. She thought, "Maybe Grandfather Makakupu convinced her to continue; after all, she did go to Ka'ū and didn't tell anyone why she was going. It seemed to be a big mystery." In her preoccupation with her thoughts, she didn't hear her daughter's questions.

"Mama, did you hear me?" shouted Kalānaue.

Startled by her daughter's voice, Lama replied, "What did you say?"

Kalānaue continued, "You think I can go to Grandma's house to listen to her chant? Maybe someone is dancing and I can watch. Also I found a book in Grandma's bedroom. There was short note on the first page and it said, 'To my mo'opuna.' Who do you think this was for?"

"Shame on you," scolded her mother. "You're not supposed to look into other people's property. Was the book open?"

With a quiet voice Kalānaue answered, "No, but do you know Grandma's old trunk? Well, it was opened and that's where I found the book."

This brought a rush of memories to Lama of her childhood days. She remembered rumbling through the trunk with her sister, mother, and grandmother. Her grandmother would pull out family and dance pictures. She kept her old hula implements in this trunk, also stories which she had written and collected. From this trunk, came stories of gods and goddesses, their love affairs and their battles.

"Mama, you're not listening again!"

"Oh, I'm sorry, but it's been fourteen years since your grandmother last opened that trunk and I'm going to find out why," said Lama.

"May I go with you, Mama?"

"No, you stay home and prepare the fish. I'm going to take half of it to Grandma."

Kai was about to sit for breakfast when Lama arrived. Lama called out, "Aloha Māmā, ihea? Where are you?"

" 'Ai ma ka lumi kuke (in the kitchen)," came the reply. "Komo mai i loko a 'ai me a'u (Come in and eat with me)," was Kai's invitation to her daughter.

Lama accepted as she had missed breakfast this morning. "We went holoholo this morning. I was 'ono for 'ohua and I brought some over for us to eat. Where is your pa'akai (salt)?"

Kai stood up to get the salt and poi. "Mahalo e Lama, he mea'ai kakahiaka 'ono kēia. Pehea 'o Naue?"[12]

"Maika'i 'o ia (She is fine)," answered Lama. "I sent her over here yesterday evening to fetch your laundry. Did you know she was here?"

" 'A'ole (no)," said Kai in surprise.

The two women commenced with their breakfast and Lama continued, "Naue said you were chanting. I thought maybe you were singing." Lama paused for her mother's reply, but Kai kept eating. "Naue said she heard you talking to someone, was anyone visiting?"

Kai shook her head and was looking a little uncomfortable. They both ate in silence, a little fish, poi, tea, and crackers.

After breakfast while they were cleaning up, Lama probed further, "How is Grandpa Makakupu in Ka'ū? And how was your visit with him?"

"Maika'i nō 'o Kūkū Makakupu, 'elemakule kona kino a ikaika ka no'ono'o."[13] After some thought she continued, " 'Ae (yes), we did have a good visit. He insisted that I continue the hula even if the dancers are not family. I talked to 'Ōlena and she suggested I teach the children of my first dancers, now they are all makua (parents), you know. So I called some and they are anxious to send their children."

---

[12] "Thanks, Lama, this is a delicious breakfast. How is Naue?"
[13] "Granduncle Makakupu is fine; his body is old but his mind is sharp."

Lama was relieved and happy that her mother wanted to move forward with something she loved so much. She felt guilty about her mother's not chanting and dancing for years. This was a little awkward because of the past; however, when she finally had enough courage, she quietly asked her mother, "Mama, you don't have to answer me now, but will you consider Naue as one of your students? I haven't taught her any hula or chants. Since that day she was born, I made an effort not to expose her to any because I felt you should be the one to teach her. This morning when she talked about hearing you chant, she was very excited and anxious to come over again and listen to you. I know you are still huhū (upset, angry) about not giving her to you, but…" Kai waved her hand for Lama to be quiet as she walked into the bedroom and sat on the bed.

Lama stood in the kitchen feeling very bad about what had just happened. She was ready to leave when Kai called her into her room and told her to sit on the bed. Lama sat on the bed on the old patch quilt she remembered her mother making a long time ago. When she looked at her mother, she noticed tears on her face and apologized, "Mama, I'm sorry, I didn't mean to hurt you again."

Kai handed a book to her daughter. When Lama opened it, she recognized the words Naue had described: "To My Moʻopuna." Kai began, "I wrote all the things I wanted to teach your daughter—there are five books. I thought I would never have the chance to teach her. When I was sixty, I could have taught her so much more. By this time she would know almost as much as I do. Your father wouldn't allow me to teach you and your sisters as much as I wanted to. You know a lot about fishing and your brother is a good farmer and ʻŌlena is a gifted lāʻau lapaʻau. These are things you learned from Pāpā's side of the family. Your father didn't think hula and chanting was important, so I didn't have the time needed to teach you children what was important in our family. My mother felt an urgency to teach our family traditions. So this created a tension between my mother and your father."

Lama listened intently because her mother had never discussed this with the family before, so she didn't interrupt as Kai continued her story: "Your grandma, Puʻuone, was very disappointed and when Kalānaue was born, I thought I would finally be able to satisfy my family's wishes. My dream of my mother and Kalānaue's birth was the key to continuing this tradition so your denial was a great blow. At that moment I was my mother, I knew and felt her disappointment. The weight of many generations was on my shoulders. The only relief for me, as small as it may be, was to write down everything I knew.

"Uncle Makakupu wrote to me a long time ago and advised me to write. When I finally finished, I went to visit him to tell him that everything was written and in order. But he insisted that I return and when the time was right, approach you and Haʻaloʻu again. And here you are!"

Kai hugged her daughter and thanked her for coming today.

At this moment, Lama understood the dilemma her mother had faced for many years. "Kalānaue is ready, Mama, and I am too. How can I help? What can I do?" asked Lama.

"We must test Naue's readiness; everything will depend on her," replied Kai.

"How can we do that, Mama?"

"Well, Uncle Makakupu asked me to send her to Kaʻū to stay with him for a while. Maybe when summer begins, we can do that. What do you think, Lama? And you have to talk it over with Haʻaloʻu first."

Lama humbly agreed with her mother. She now realized her mother's predicament. Many thoughts raced through her mind. How can she approach her husband? Will he understand this urgency her mother is feeling? Naue has never been away before, will she hesitate about going away? How will she feel about staying with someone she doesn't know? So many things to work out. Lama couldn't remember her parting comments to her mother, when she thought about it she was already home.

That evening at dinner, Naue blurted out to her mother, "Was Grandma chanting today? Did you see the things in her trunk? Did you ask who was visiting her and why she was beating the ipu? Is Grandma a good chanter? I never heard her before this, why?"

Haʻaloʻu was totally surprised at his daughter's rapid questioning and even more surprised at what she was asking. "What are you talking about, Naue?"

Naue was more than happy to share her excitement with her father. "Well, yesterday…" she went on to explain the whole thing to her father almost in one breath.

Haʻaloʻu turned to his wife with a quizzical look and asked, "What is this all about, Lama? Is the problem from her birth surfacing?"

"I'll explain to you after dinner, and Naue, we'll discuss this with you after we talk," was Lama's firm answer. After this, dinner was completed in silence.

Lama and Haʻaloʻu sat on the porch that evening while Naue cleaned the kitchen. A little wind was blowing and the moon was in its Hua phase (13th moon phase of Hawaiian month, the fruiting phase). Lama thought, "This is a good time to begin a new cycle in our lives." She commenced to tell her husband about the things which took place within the last two days. When she finished, she waited for his comments and thoughts.

He started with "Who is Uncle Makakupu? I've never heard you talk about him. What makes him so special that your mother would listen to him? She doesn't listen to anyone else!"

"Uncle Makakupu is my mother's uncle. He is the hiapo of Grandma Puʻuone's family. He must be over a hundred years old because my mother is seventy-four. The family said that he is a kāula (seer, prophet) and yet he is a very humble man. He knows a lot about the old things and ways and is well respected by his family and all those who know him. I've only met him twice. I don't know anything else about him."

"Is he married? Does he have children or grandchildren? Do you want Naue to go off and live with him? How long will she be there?"

"All I know, Haʻaloʻu, is what I heard when I was a child that he lived alone most of his life. He did have a wife but they didn't have any children. When she died he chose to live alone. In answer to your other question, my mother didn't know how long Naue would be there in Kaʻū. However, I really want Naue to learn to dance and chant from my mother. My mother is getting old and it seems like this is the last chance Naue has to learn from my mother. I want to trust my mother's judgement, Haʻaloʻu."

"This is very difficult for me, Lama, but we've enjoyed our daughter for fourteen years. At this time of her life, I think we can share her with your mother. I know this will make your mother happy. I feel proud that your mother is looking to Naue to continue this tradition of her family. I would like to entrust the care of our daughter to your mother. And I don't think we have a choice in this matter."

Lama was overwhelmed by her husband's wisdom and his quick consent to Naue's journey. Lama was hugging her husband when Naue walked onto the lanai.

"It looks like you two are celebrating. Tell me the good news!" pleaded Naue.

"Sit down, Naue, and I'll tell you," Lama commenced with the story from the beginning with Kaipalaoa's dream, Makakupu, and finally their decision for Naue to live with him for a while, then return to dance with her grandmother.

Naue's eyes sparkled as she looked forward to this new adventure with her grandmother Kaipalaoa.

Three months later—

Naue and Lama were up early in the morning and were packing food and clothing. They packed the car until it had no more room. This was the day Naue was going to go to Ka'ū for her visit with Kūkū Makakupu. And everyone was excited.

Naue had been spending a lot of time with her grandmother, who was almost a stranger to her three months ago. She had learned some oli, hula, and listened to the stories of the family, of Pelehonuamea (the goddess of volcanic activities and all other things connected to the volcano), of the great mudflow of 1868, and of this mysterious great-grandfather[14] she was about to visit. She was a little worried and wanted to ask questions but there didn't seem to be enough time. And now, they were heading down south to Ka'ū.

It seemed like they were driving for hours before Lama directed her husband off the main highway as they made their way past a little town, then out towards the valley. They drove in silence for several miles, not minding the old dirt road. They were attracted by the large cliff covered with trees which seemed to be getting bigger and bigger as they got closer. There was a dark cloud looming over the valley and the cliff ahead and Ha'alo'u was a little worried.

"How much farther?" asked Ha'alo'u.

"I'm not sure, just keep driving till I see something familiar," said Lama.

"There's sure a lot of sugar cane," thought Naue. "He doesn't live in the cane field, does he?" she asked.

"No, he lives at the base of that large hill with trees around him," was Lama's reply. "There it is! See that house up there in front of the trees? That's his house. Drive up that road, Ha'alo'u," Lama said as she pointed up the hill.

As they drove closer, they noticed a figure of a man standing on the dirt road outside the house. "It's him, it's Kūkū Makakupu!" Lama waved frantically to him.

---

[14] Western practice differentiates between a father and an uncle; Hawaiian practice does not. The generation is important.

"Oh my, he looks exactly as I remember him twenty or so years ago. He hasn't changed. Look at his long white beard and hair!"

Makakupu stood outside his house by the front gate dressed in denim shirt and long sleeve sweater, a pair of riding pants, and riding boots. He looked like something from the old pictures they had seen in the trunk. His eyes peered out from under his thick eyebrows and his nose was red from the coolness of the valley air. His hands were large and he stood with his back straight. He was a formidable figure, looking like he was at least six feet tall. There was nothing gentle about this man.

When Haʻaloʻu stopped the car, Lama ran out to honi (kiss or touch noses) her grandfather whom she had not seen for years. They held each other for a long time as Haʻaloʻu and Naue stood by the car.

"E Lama, ʻo ʻoe kā! Kū ʻoe i kou Tūtū, ʻo Puʻuone. Hauʻoli au e ʻike iā ʻoe,"[15] said Makakupu in his deep guttural voice. "I can see your grandmother in your smile, eyes, and face, and even the way you kick out your toes when you walk."

Lama smiled and said, "E Kūkū, eia koʻu ʻohana."[16] As Lama turned to her family, Naue began chanting to her great grandfather:

Aia i ka maka a ka pali,
Uhi ka makani maka lihi pali aku,
Ke lūlū aʻe nei i nā pua lehua,
Pā mai ma ka ʻaʻaliʻi,
Kū ka ʻaʻaliʻi o Kaʻū ika makani kū.
Ke kupu nei i ka palikū,
Na wai ke kupu ʻo ʻoe?
ʻO kuʻu maka kupu o Kaʻū
ʻEō mai ʻo Makakupu kou inoa.

There in the face of the cliff,
The wind spreads beyond the cliff,
Scattering the lehua blossoms.

---

[15] "Lama, it's indeed you. You have a strong resemblance to your grandmother, Puʻuone. I'm happy to see you."
[16] "Great granduncle, here is my family."

It touches the 'a'ali'i.
The 'a'ali'i stands in the stiff wind
Sprouting in the tall cliff.
Whose sprout are you?
My favorite sprout of Ka'ū
Answer, Makakupu is your name.

Makakupu, as if expecting this call, immediately replied:

Aia ka lā i ka hikina
Ma ka umauma a ka moana,
Ke naue luna nei i ka manawa,
Ke 'ōku'u nei i ka nu'u,
Na wai i naue ka lā?
Na Kalānaueikalani,
'Eō mai kou inoa.

The sun is in the east
On the breast of the ocean
It is moving above the head
Sitting at the apex.
Who is the one who moves the sun?
It is Kalānaueikalani
Answer to your name.

Naue continued her chant:

Eia nōō,
He 'umeke ka'ele
No ka ho'opihapiha 'ana
Ke 'imi nei i ka mea'ai.

Here indeed is
An empty calabash
to be filled

It is in search of food.

Makakupu responded quickly:

Aia ka meaʻai i ke awāwa
i ke kai, ika hale laʻa o Pele
i ka wao nahele.
Inā hāmama nō ka ʻumeke
Alaila, e hoʻopihapiha me ka mea ola!

The food is in the valley,
In the sea, in the sacred house of Pele,
In the forest.
If the calabash is indeed open
Then fill it with life-giving substance!

Lama and Haʻaloʻu were awe-struck by the exchange between their very young daughter and this very old grandfather. All doubts of their daughter's stay in Kaʻū vanished. Naue was ready for this responsibility and there were no questions in their minds, only encouragement.

After Makakupu and Kalānaue embraced, the great-grandfather took the hands of his moʻopunahine kuakahi (great-granddaughter) and pointed out towards the east, "Aia lā ʻo Pele. I ka lā ʻapōpō, e hele aku kāua ma leila. Pono kāua e hoʻomākaukau i kēia manawa."[17]

Upon hearing this, Lama smiled to herself and turned to Haʻaloʻu and said, "Well, our daughter is in good hands. It's time for us to go home!"

"We were going to leave tomorrow, Lama!"

"They are going to be too busy to bother with us. This is a beginning for our daughter, Haʻaloʻu, but almost the end for Kūkū Makakupu and I can feel that he is anxious to start with Naue's initiation and introduction to the kūpuna."

And so, Lama and Haʻaloʻu bade farewell to Kūkū Makakupu and their daughter knowing they would see her soon.

---

[17] "Pele is there. Tomorrow we are going there. We must prepare now."

NOTE: For additional information and some insights on the author, see interview by Lorilani Keohokalole on page 118.

Cocktail Waitress Series

❦ Tamara Laulani Wong-Morrison ❦

Koa canoe, you slant on your side
Mounted in hotel dining room,
Listening to pre-recorded Polynesian songs
Playing over and over
While I cocktail wait on hungry tourists.
Herb Kane oil painting adorn you—finely done;
Strange Hawaiian in a foreign place.
"Kaulana Nā Pua," they play from your recorder.
They do not know the meaning of eating from the stones
Instead of signing the papers of the enemy.

Me, local lady must wear flower in hair because the
Management says so.
Right or left side over my ear—I do not care.
All I want from you Haole is your money
In return for some plastic Aloha,
Smiles I do not mean,
Warmness that is actually cold.
Drink my chi-chis and mai-tais that
I cover with paper umbrellas from Hong Kong.
See this paradise through glazed eyes.
I know of a better way.
I am selfish though.
Your taking has taught me to be shrewd.

Here we are: Japanese bus-boy, Haole waiter separated from
Filipino wife – working two jobs to pay mortgage and rent
With one pay check.
Four dollars in tips tonight.

Proper Offerings to Pele

⋙ TAMARA LAULANI WONG-MORRISON ⋘

Don't throw gin as your offering to Pele,
You drink it, she prefers your first ʻōhelo berries,
Red bulbs complete with an offering chant.
And if you don't know the chant,
Be silent or learn it,
Don't make it up.
Such creativity is reserved for the learned ones
Whose minds remember forty-thousand lines in one breath.

Don't burn prayer papers for Pele,
Your slanted-eyed spirits are the only ones who can read them.
They are many miles from here,
This crater's edge is not their temple.
Your burned paper and incense smoke singed with sulphur,
Useless.

A steamed pig would do,
She'll like that; Kamapuaʻa on a platter.
Her beloved enemy that eats away at her,
Carves deep valleys into her,
Continually consuming,
She'll savor him.

And if a pig is too big,
Offer a weke ʻula, wide-eyed red fish, fresh--
Wrap him in ti leaves.

Calvary at 'Anaeho'omalu

❧ Mahealani Perez-Wendt (formerly Kamauu) ☙

In a hotel lobby
Near 'Anaeho'omalu Bay
A resort manager's grand idea
Of Christmas in Hawai'i--

A two-story Norfolk
Festooned with implements
Of Hawaiian dance:
Feather gourds, 'ulī'ulī,
Gaily colored and fastened
With braided hau;
Double gourds, ipu heke,
Suspended by intricate netting;
Split bamboo, pū'ili,
Backdrop of kapa--
All gifts from an
Ancient intelligence,
The whole show
Razzle dazzle electric,
Undulating, haole hula,
To soft offshore breezes.
I stand at Christ's tree,
And from another temple
Illuminated by oils of kukui hele pō
And the moon goddess Hina,
An intoxication of holy communion:
From a stranger's silver chalice pours
The dark blood of ancestors.

Pulsating
Blood and sinew
Sensate with the drumming of pahu,
Clash of ka lāʻau,
Rattle of kūpeʻe,
Rapping of ipu heke;
Voices rise out of shadow
And intone an ancient cadence:

E Laka e	(Oh Laka)
Pūpū weuweu	(Oh wild wood bouquet)
E Laka e	(Oh Laka)
ʻAnoʻi aloha e	(Greetings and salutations)
ʻAnoʻi aloha e	(Greetings and salutations)
ʻAnoʻi aloha e	(Greetings and salutations)

In a hotel lobby
ʻAnaehoʻomalu spinning,
I feel tethered and hammered through,
Wild among dark branches
Snared by voices on angry winds.

Max was hea

❧ CATHY KANOELANI IKEDA ❧

Stolen Gargoyle glasses
Hide your bloodshot eyes.
We sit in your '64
Lime-green Bug.
A faded blue and white tassle,
Hanging on your rear-view mirror,
Trembles as the rap,
Onyx with heavy bass,
Spills into the glare of noon.
Your vacant eyes stare at the surf.
I think you're dead,
Just sitting there
As a cigarette threatens to burn your fingers.
"What's wrong?" I ask.
You say nothing for what seems like forever,
More like three sets.
I have nothing better to do,
I count the waves
And try not to go deaf.
Then your petroglyph tattoo moves.
You turn the tape down,
and your voice, so serene in the
Violent ringing of my ears tells me,
"Life's fucked!
I thought everything was going be so simple,
Surf, cruise, party, surf again
Just the way we dreamed about, remember?
But I neva dream about this.
You saw Joey Wong's picture in the paper?
The one that talk about doctors they get

At their hospital?

Kaiser or something?

Joey, the one Andy wen corner in the bathroom

5th grade time

And Joey wen get so scared he piss his pants

'Ass how come we used to call him

shishi boy in high school.

He one fricken obstetrician,

Then get Randy, he playing pro ball

Up the mainland someplace,

And Tammie, the one we call giraffe

Stay modeling in Paris

And I see her in the Liberty House

Catalogs sometimes, Zooper sale, li' dat.

And then get Lei,

The one who asked Michael to the prom

Then Paka boy, then Scotty

And she wen get rejected by all of them,

How the fuck we knew she would be Miss Hawai'i?

She neva look like that in high school.

Andy, he the lucky one, though

Cause wen his car wen huli

Wrap around the banyan tree,

Crash and burn,

At least was one week after graduation,

And everybody wen come out

And we knew he was gone

Scattered his ashes in the ocean

J'like he was one Viking or something.

But nobody told me that

I would still be living in Waimānalo,

Same house, same room

My mother doing my laundry

And bitchin at me about finding one job

And keeping em.

Nobody told me

All my dreaming wasn't going be enough

And after ten years of this shit

It ain't enough

And I stay lost

Like going disappear in the foam

And nobody going give a fuck,

No one going know I gone."

I want to say something funny,

Or something profound

Something that will make you snap out of it,

But all I can think about is you.

20 years ago,

You were in warp speed, telling us

About the newest Kikaida show

With spit flying you jumped on the table,

Showed us how Kikaida threw his death kick

Arms taut in the death chop,

Your bare feet flying high in the air

Shattering the glass door

Your rusty blood spilled on the yellow sidewalk,

And I cried for you, the pool spreading

My salty tears mixing with yours

As I took my finger, stirred it in your crimson blood

And wrote, "Max was hea"

On the once virgin glass.

You fumble for another tape.

Bring me forward 20 years,

Two friends sharing a smoke.

Through the haze,

The swirl of dust you tell me,

"I scared shitless
Get nightmares of being my pops,
Beer gut hanging out the bottom of his shirt
His pants so fuckin low
You can see his crack when he standing up.
I see him under the mango tree
Drinkin beer with all the other losers
All day, all night
And mom no say nothin to him
'Cause at least he get his workman's comp check.
Plus I think she just fuckin bitched out already
'Cause bitchin at him j'like yelling at the ocean
You get drowned out by his snores,
So she working on me,
Hoping I neva go deaf yet
Too late.
I can think about all the things I shoulda done
All the times I had the chance
And neva take 'em
But everything is past already,
Too late,
And if all I get in front of me is my pops
Wearing the same undershirt
Every damn day

The thing so thin can see right through,
Too late,
And that perfect wave,
The one we dreamed about,
The tube we said was like heaven
And sex
Sucked me under
And I neva even know until stay
Too late."

I don't know how to bring you back
Or tell you what you mean to me.
I take out some lipstick,
Brandied Berry 71
And write,
"Max is hea."

"Max" was written for my students at Hilo High [she is now teaching at Kamehameha School, Hawai'i]. Max is a wake up call for my students who think that what they are now is what they're going to be forever. Max is for the nerd in the library, the clown, the prom queen, the jock, the bully and all the Maxes that think that no one will care if they just disappear.

[This appeared previously in "Authors' Notes," *Growing Up Local: an anthology of poetry and prose from Hawai'i*, Edited by Eric Chock, James R. Harstad, Darrell H.Y. Lum & Bill Teter, Honolulu: Bamboo Ridge Press, 1998, 361.]

Queenie

❧ Mahealani Perez-Wendt (formerly Kamauu) ☙

My name is Queenie
I am a direct lineal descendant
Of Queen Ka'ahumanu
I just found this out
I researched the Archives
Everywhere I did my research
I never found this out
Until one day I talked to
That lady--you know her--
Always hanging around there--
She knows all about
The genealogies
She told me "Queenie,
That boy Martin
You know him
He's a big shot
That's Auntie Katie's boy
From Kaua'i
They related to you
They have information
About your genealogy
When I talked to them
I went to Kaua'i
And I found out
About being royal blood
I just cried
I couldn't tell anybody
Who could I tell?
I just cried, I tell you

I went into the forest
By myself
And I cried
To the trees
They understood
Our kūpuna
Received me
And they wen understand me
Who else could I tell?
Nobody.
I tell you
I cried and cried.
So you see
What I am telling you
Is the truth.
My ancestors were ali'i
They were of
The royal class
That's why I
Cannot put up
With squatters
On my land.

Who are these people?
They have no rights!
They don't belong
On this land.
This is my land.
This is a place
Where the King himself
Used as a retreat;
The King himself!
Where you can find

Anybody who can say
That their tūtū
Was invited
Into the compound
Of the aliʻi?
You cannot find that.
But I remember
This place
Since I was a child.
A little girl.
When was low tide
My tūtū man
Would carry me
On his shoulders
To that island.
Who the hell
Are these people
To come here and squat?
They're nobody! They're
Commoner class. I am an
Aliʻi. I tell you the
Truth, if my tūtū man were
Alive today, they would never,
They would never, treat me
This way!

Who are these people?
What right do they have here?
They don't own this land.
This land belongs to my family.
They had a
What you call
Condemnation.

Actually,
I got no beef with
The state.
The federal wen take 'em.
First during the war
Then they wen give 'em
To the state.
What right did they have to
Take our land?
Fuck the United States!

Fuck them all.
My friends tell me
"Queenie, you get all
the rights. You should
fight for the island. You
know that belongs to you."
And I tell them, "I know."
I tell you true
I not going rest
Until I get justice.
Who are these people
To come here and
Act like they own the land?
My grandfather sued for
The island--
Incomplete, he died.
They did a fraud.
My grandfather was
The first to put in
His claim. When my tūtū died
Nobody dared touch
That island.

When I speak
It comes out
Spiritually.
My name is Queenie.
I like to declare war
On the United States.
And I tell them too.
When I say this
They must be thinking
Wow, she must be a Communist.
But the U.S.
Know they cannot
Get away with this.
They know Queenie
Can prove the genealogy
They know I'm
Going to bring the lawsuit
Even the Campbells
Cannot prove anything.
You know what my real
Name is? Kahuionalani Kupihea.
It hurts, it still hurts.
But I will carry this fight
Until I die.
They take one look at me
I look so dumb
I speak pidgin English
I want to act mean too
Like my kings and queens
In a spiritual way
When I meditate or chant
Things come right for me
But I tell you

The way I feel
I like kill somebody
I like kill all of them
They trying to make
The Hawaiians mentally ill
You know my friends tell me
Let's go down there
And blow everything up.

Pity

❧ CATHY KANOELANI IKEDA ☙

No 'i been living on the beach
Four years now
All the 'ohana camped out
Semi-permanent blue-tarped houses
Living off the 'āina
That belong to them
Stolen by the haoles,
Unable to cope with a philosophy
Foreign to the kanaka—time, money
Ownership, property.
He say, "better to live down Onekahakaha
Take a crap in the county toilets,
Fish by the county sewer
Live off the haole government
Who stole the 'āina
From the Hawaiians
'Cause if you collect welfare,
AFDC, food stamps, WIC
'Ass like paying 'em back, eh?"

Generations of Hawaiians
Getting back at the white men
By taking their hand-outs
And flying the Hawaiian flag,
        the one copied from the other white men
        far across the sea
        on another island,
Upside down,

A sign of distress.
The newest political vocabulary word
All Hawaiians know next to Sovereignty--
Distress, auwē...auwē
Pity us,
Restitution,
We not going follow your laws,
'Cause we part of the sovereign nation,
But no stop the welfare checks,
'Cause we forgot how for grow the essential kalo
Sacred green and brown like the earth
Harvested from the 'āina,
And we forgot how to catch the wily he'e
Caught in the gleaming cowry shells
And we forgot the old songs for praising our ancestors,
And we forgot the words for the wind
And we forgot how to brew the bitter medicine
And we go to school to learn the language
We once knew from before birth,
'Ōlelo Hawai'i,
And our grandfathers' names are untranslatable
In this modern, Anglicized, unemotional language.

We forgot
Because of the pasty white men with no breath
The half-dead ghosts--ha 'ole.

But we really forgot
Because we were stupid
We forgot because we couldn't keep our people out of jail,
We couldn't keep our parents from beating our kids,
We couldn't keep the alcohol and pakalolo out of our blood system,
We couldn't adapt.

We couldn't haul our heads up out of our ass,
We could only give up, talk shit
And forget.
Auwē.

Can You Feel

❧ RELYN TIMBAL ☙
Written while a high school student at Kamehameha School

Can you feel your heart begin to race
The burn run down your throat
The fire in your stomach
Your body begin to sweat?
Well, go ahead and sip again, young Hawaiian

Can you feel the warmth overtake you
The dizziness in your head
The world begin to dance
The high that's in your mind?
Well, sniff again, young Hawaiian

Can you feel the colors getting brighter
Your mind begins to wander
The urge getting stronger?
Well, hit again, young Hawaiian

Can you feel your body begin to weaken
Your life begin to crumble
The sickness in your stomach
The hand of death reaching you?
Well, kill yourself, young Hawaiian
Just like the rest of them.

My Bus Is Two Hours Late

≫ MAHEALANI PEREZ-WENDT (FORMERLY KAMAUU) ≪

Jack-in-the-Box smiles lurid
Through smoke-colored glass;
A midnight apparition in neon,
Formless and vaporized
At the Union Mall bus stop.
I'm a 99-Cent Special
Hanging with Jack,
A penitent for life
Consigned to streetcorner ʻukulele
And preacher's admonitions
Against Satan and his angels.
I'm a matron once a maid,
Lights gone out
With the one zillionth
Dream vacationer who,
Having luxuriated between
Hotel sheets
And a full measure
Of room service
Has gone,
Leaving me vacant,
Rank and unmade.
I sink quietly to knees
In the place prepared
By Jack's Faithful.
I kneel among rancid offerings:
Paper cups, cigarettes,
Garbage strewn about
The silent streets.
I pray for lost sons

Struck senseless and star-crossed
By spirits;
For old men convulsive
In dirty felt hats;
For the hospital freed
Doing the thorazine shuffle;
I pray for preacher
Whose 'ukulele scriptures
Are Satan's bus stop nemesis;
For old ladies
Worrying behind
Grey spectacles
Fumbling at the pay phone
And giving up.
I pray for all
Seeking light
Missing important signposts
And going up in smoke.
Theirs are the voices
Of soft restraint
Whispering to the driver
Their wait has been long.
Jack-in-the-Box smiles lurid
Through smoke-colored glass;
A midnight apparition in neon,
Formless and vaporized
At the Union Mall bus stop.
I'm a graveyard shift conscript
Hanging with Jack
Going with his angels
For one last ride.

Retaliation

❧ JACKIE PUALANI JOHNSON ❧

I could spit in the colonist's face
Spray paint his rental car with juicy aspersions
Dripping with pointed, poignant Pidgin
Or lean out the car window at Hapuna
And call "You fuckin' haole"
When he makes a wrong turn at an unfamiliar intersection
Or----
I could choose more insidious weapons
        Ka 'ōlelo makuahine[18]
        Ka loina Hawai'i[19]
        Ho'okūpono[20]
To chip away his chokehold on my na'au
Liberate me from the blinding anger
That keeps me locked in self pity
Over the shame of having to learn
How to be Hawaiian
Again.

---

[18] ka 'ōlelo makuahine: mother tongue
[19] ka loina Hawai'i: Hawaiian culture
[20] ho'okūpono: proceeding correctly, "doing it right"

Pele's Last Rainforest
(FOR 'ŪLĀLEO WHO SPOKE OUT FOR HIS FIERY 'AUMAKUA)

❧ PHYLLIS COOCHIE CAYAN ❧

Auwē! Wao Kele o Puna,
the white man ways demand
your spiritual end.

The lush 'ōhi'a forest nurtures
its rare plant life,
her silence stabbed by a drilling knife.

Tutu awakens at Pu'u 'O'ō,
her anger creates sacred land,
She scorns the evils of man.

The flowing, groaning 'āina
shifts its hot magma waves,
crackling through miles of secret caves.

Go and tell the story,
Pele's last rainforest is not for sale or rent.
Auwē! Wao Kele o Puna, auwē!

The Birth of Moʻomomi

ッ TOLD BY RACHELLE MAIKUI ৵
Transcribed by Esther Figueroa

Was March 26, 1991. Upon waking that morning I received a spiritual manaʻo to come to Moʻomomi to ʻauʻaukai, to bathe in the sea. So my Papa prepared the truck and we proceeded to come down here. Along the routes, I could feel all of the ʻohana on both sides of the truck, the entire distance. Up there, there is this pua kala that's been a guardian of this area for many, many years. When we reached that point, out here on the bay, there was a mama whale and a calf. Immediately I was filled with joy and said, "Papa, hōʻailona, hōʻailona" (which means a good sign). So we came down and upon entering Moʻomomi Bay, here his Mama and his family was right behind us and my ʻohana was camping there so it was quite a meeting of ʻohana. Then we proceeded over there where is our beach hale and the family joined us and we all had lunch. Then the family left and it was time. So I told "Dad, it's time to go ʻauʻau," so he blew the conch shell, the pū. So proceeded down the side of the cliff kāhea all the way down.

Then I disrobed down by the pōhaku by the sea and I was gracefully seated amongst the pōhaku and that felt like a beautiful, comfortable chair. As I awaited, the waves came upon me like fingers caressing my body, washing me from head to toe with such gentleness. When it was done, gracefully I was stood so that I knew that all of the ʻohana with much aloha were present. Then I took a few steps back and Papa was there with the fresh water to rinse me, pat me dry, and put my pareau back on. Then we proceeded back up to the hale. We were busy just enjoying the scenery. Then he told me, "Well, Mama, before the sun go down, we go," and then I said, "Oh! Auwē! Here comes the water!" So I needed to walk the whole fronting of our hale, drop by drop, step by step, the water upon the ʻāina. Then my ʻōpū came to a big swell with no pain.

Then I said, "Oh, Daddy, baby wanna be born here." "Okay. Okay." So we waited, then I got down on the beach mat on the sand. Then he tells me, "Oh Mama, what we gonna cut the piko, the cord, with?" Then I am reminded did not the Akua send me to the drug store get a first aid kit for the truck? "Go get it." So he goes and gets in and there the scissors! Bambai he ask, "What we going use to tie?" I'm on the ground. I look up at him and say, "Ah, Dad! You will know." Sure enough. "Ah, I wait." He runs to the truck where he gets his net needle that he just put on cotton thread. Ai, that is good. So we await. Then as I go into labour and I go backwards on my back arching, above under the palm trees there is this diamond opening. I can see the moon, so I tell him, "Daddy, when this moon directly in this opening, baby he come!" Sure enough, here comes the moon. I can see it clearly. I say, "Daddy, come, come, Baby coming." Ah, poop, out comes the baby—beautiful boy. So I tell him, "Daddy, you have to suck the hūpē from the nose." So he says, "Heh?" So I say, "If you can't do it, pass Baby! Pass Baby!" But the cord is not far enough for me to reach the baby. So I tell him, "You must do it, now!" So he does, he sucks the nose and says, "Ah, da sweet!" And I say, "Good, good!"

The baby is totally clean, no blood, no matter upon him, and he gives quite a yell which made us feel very happy. For many, many years these valleys down here have not heard the cry of a new born. It was quite an experience!

Then on the third day his piko fell off, so I said, "Ah, Daddy, time for Moʻomomi, which we named him, to be brought back down here for his first bath. So we proceeded very ceremonial and there is on the beach a bath tub in the pōhaku and there is also another pōhaku where you place the piko and put your own pōhaku on top. So Daddy went with his pū and went to the sea. He bring back water, clean the pōhaku, then put fresh sea water and let the sun warm it up and he handled all of the bathing. I just stood by. And it was quite an experience.

So, yes, Moʻomomi means very much to me and my ʻohana and that child carries the name of Moʻomomi. That boy is five years old today and he's a kindergartner in Kula Kaiapuni at Kualapuʻu School. And his name is Nakaiʻilimokuku keikikaniʻomoʻomomi, which is very befitting that child.

EPILOGUE: The Passing of Moʻomomi

It is fitting that Anake Snookie's story of the Birth of Moʻomomi be completed by the Passing of Moʻomomi. On March 25, 2008, one day before his 17th birthday, Moʻomomi died in a car crash. Various hōʻailona marked his passing as they did his birth. As Moʻomomi's ashes were taken to the sea and Anake Snookie blew the conch shell sending her ha with a prayer, Kumu Karen Kamalu Poepoe chanted her composition, "Ke One Hūnā o Moʻomomi,"* of which the last three stanzas (compressed) follow:

The hiding white sands of Keonelele flee
Standing naked in the bone revealing wind
The ʻiwa bird returns to the perches of Kukaemanu
The place unhidden to those who belong.
The native sons return to the dunes of Moʻomomi,
Embraced in the heart, the native sons of Molokai.

The Molokai Times reported that "as his ashes were placed into the bay at the spot of his birth…An unexpected rain appeared for a few minutes only to give way again to a warm bright sun."

Anake Snookie said that next day when his birthday party began, a white owl flew by. Her search for the proper ipu gourd for his ashes ended when she found one with the face of a white owl.

******

*Kumu Poepoe had composed the chant in 1991, but, according to her, it "went into hiding and came out when Moʻo passed."

NOTE: For additional information and some insights on the author and on the work, see interview by Flora Collins on page 113.

Strange Scent 1978

❧ TAMARA LAULANI WONG-MORRISON ☙

Hear the beating of the pahu drum
Distant and warning,
Beware,
      A strange wave has washed upon the rocks,
Even the crabs run from their homes
In the night it passed over shining black water,
Gliding, not knowing where it came from or where it's going,
An omnipresence—there.
Me, I tried to sleep under a starless sky,
But too dark, too strange, too still.
I feel I will never be the same again.

January 1978, Hawai'i's "Bicentennial"

Uluhaimalama [1]

❧ Mahealani Perez-Wendt (formerly Kamauu) ❧

We have gathered
With manacled hands;
We have gathered
With shackled feet;
We have gathered
In the dust of forget
Seeking the vein
Which will not collapse.
We have bolted
The gunner's fence,
Given sacrament
On blood-stained walls.
We have linked souls
End to end
Against the razor's slice.
We have kissed brothers
In frigid cells,
Pressing our mouths
Against their ice-hard pain.
We have feasted well
On the stones of the land [2]
We have gathered
In dark places

---

[1] Uluhaimalama: The name of Queen Lili'uokalani's garden. The kaona, or meaning, of that word is that as plants grow up out of the dark into the light, so shall light come to the Hawaiian nation.

[2] Feasting on stones is a reference to Kaulana Nā Pua, the song of protest written after the overthrow of the Hawaiian Nation. In it, the songwriter says that Hawaiians would rather eat stones than accept any annexationist proffer.

And put down roots.
We have covered the Earth,
Bold flowers for her crown.
We have climbed
The high wire of treason--
We will not fall.

Written in honor of Queen Liliʻuokalani on the anniversary of her birthday.

Braddah

❧ PHYLLIS COOCHIE CAYAN ❧

My braddah take me beach,
    Teach me how to fish
       And throw net.

My braddah sit and look
    Out to sea,
Talk about sovereignty.

My braddah told me,
No change for nobody.
Stay Hawaiian.

My braddah no stay,
They take him away,
All day rainy.

Native Hawaiian in Prison
(The Blue Light)

❧ Mahealani Perez-Wendt (formerly Kamauu) ❧

As a boy in Nuʻuanu
He heard the Ancients whisper.
His mother, who did not hear them
Made sure he placed the maile
By their marble crypts.
Red ginger lauaʻe,
Carried in heavy buckets,
Sloshing through underground chambers,
Paths of light going up,
Dark paths going down.

He swam at Kapena,
A young boy's reward.
At these times his heart sang
For the high waterfall,
The Ancients in his ear,
The slippery climb up,
The arcing dive down.

He tended the fires of peace;
He saw the Lord on Sunday,
A whipping on Monday.
On other days he saw other things--
When the Ancients whisper,
Who can know the heart of a boy?

In time he was sent away
To better love the Lord.

He was sent
To not where
Sweet hallelujah
Was a needle's high
And glory glory
A spreading thigh.

The Ancients came again.
This time they baptized him
In their own way.
At Nāpoʻopoʻo

His heart was a drum:
He danced with ʻIolani
The white sacred bird.
The next time they whispered
He swam with manō.
His heart sang
For this boy's reward;
The green world below, The blue light above.
Prison is a place
Where the Ancients are silenced,
And Earth's song
Cannot be heard
It is a crypt
Beyond breathing
Flowerless, without life's fragrance.

The boy sits in a cell
Far from the white bird's cry
With the incandescent hum
Of blue light from above.

*More than 60% of all prison inmates in Hawai'i are Native Hawaiian.
Hawaiians love the ocean…I was thinking about sunlight through blue
water and about prison cells where blue electric lights are electronically
controlled to stay on all the time. I was feeling blue about free-spirited
Hawaiians suffocating in a place where the sun never shines—*

Inspirational Radio

⅌ CHERYL BAUTISTA ⅌
Written while a high school student at Kamehameha School

As I sit here,
listening to the Hawaiian radio station,
the songs take me back to the past
Where the songs, the language, the culture
like the Hawaiian people themselves,
were almost wiped out.
Why?
Was it for my ancestors'
innocence?
For their naiveté?
Or because the weather here
was too perfect
and they needed to suffer somehow.

But as I whip back into reality,
I realize that I have nothing to worry about.
Like the comforting hands on an aching body,
My conscience reminds me
that I'm living proof of the
Hawaiian spirit.
Even though the tag
on the back of my shirt may not say
100% KAPA,
I know the Hawaiian spirit lives
in me.
And I must be honest,
I'm a little shaky on
the idea of sovereignty,

But that doesn't make me
any less of a Hawaiian.
As a Hawaiian
I will do everything
to make sure this Hawaiian spirit
lives on
like those songs
on the radio.

Hoʻoulu Lāhui

✒ VICTORIA NALANI KNEUBUHL ✒

At dawn the chanting called Kahikina out of sleep. She sat up and parted the bedroom curtains from her upstairs window. No, she wasn't dreaming, he was still there. Only the wooden gate separated him from the stone path which led up to her door, but she knew he would never come across unless she chanted back to him with her kāhea, welcoming him in the formal and polite way of their ancestors. Unless she did so, the flimsy wooden gate might just as well have been a forty-foot moat swimming with sharks and poisonous water snakes. She could see him clearly, his white hair, his tall figure against the voluminous morning, his vibrant breath rising in his chest and falling out through his voice in rich, dark tones.

Anger pricked at the back of her neck. What the hell does he expect? Her thoughts came fast and loud. Three days and he's still out there thinking I might welcome him in. Why should I? I don't even know him. I don't even want to know him. Let him wait. Let him wait forever or go back to where he came from. It's all too ludicrous.

Kahikina sat at the edge of the bed swinging her feet in opposite circles and stared at the floor. She stood up, grabbed her robe from the chair and shuffled downstairs to the kitchen. While she waited for the water to boil, she brushed out her long dark hair with its streaks of white running through it like messy pin stripes. She'd thought about taking the pill, the gene therapy pill that would keep her hair its natural color forever. She'd already surrendered to the same kind of treatment for aging skin, but Kahikina wanted the gray in her hair. She liked having a sign that announced the kind of maturity she felt she earned after 67 years of living. She braided up the variegated tresses, twirled them around and secured them with a wooden hair pick, carved in the shape of a lizard, at the back of her neck.

The man at the gate began chanting about Papa and Wākea. Papa, the earth mother, and Wākea, the sky father, progenitors of the Hawaiian race. Kahikina listened and for a minute mused over his version. I guess he never heard the old story, the way it was told before the Ministry of Hawaiian Culture shaped oral history. "Kanaka nouveau," grandma used to call the proud new bureaucrats. But I remember hearing a different story, from grandma's lips, along, in secret. "And don't tell mommie," she always said.

That was Kahikina's first year in school, the year 2021 when Ke Aupuni Hou Hawai'i, the New Hawaiian Nation, was only ten years old. She used to think her grandmother made up that story. It was certainly different from the one she learned in school, but now it all made sense. Yes, there was a great darkness. And in that darkness there were great shadows, and in the shadows dirty hands sealed secret deals—without the knowledge or consent of those whose lives their plans would splinter. His chant was closing and Kahikina could almost feel the calling in his life breath like the smoke of a genie spiraling back into a bottle. Yes, she thought, he has a voice.

Kahikina knew she must have met him at some time in her life. He's about her age and looks full blooded, kanaka maoli piha. All the families met every year at the counsel when she was growing up. They were only a handful by then. At the time the new nation was formed, pure Hawaiians had dwindled to 300 men, women, and children. The first sovereign parliament set aside the best land for them, subsidized their housing, provided educational benefits, job counseling, training, and complete medical care. The medical programs were the most intensive. They conducted bi-yearly physical examinations, monitoring diet, weight, and exercise every month on a compulsory basis until the age of 18 when the program became voluntary. However, almost all of the other benefits required "voluntary" participation in the medical programs, so the routine continued. They checked everything—eyes, ears, lungs, blood, heart, piss, everything, all the time. They must have watched her for a long time.

It didn't seem so strange then. She'd grown up being treated like an extraordinary bird of a rare and endangered species. All of them were subjected to the poking and prodding, but as if in return, they were always given the best, always an honored place at ceremonies, always invited to every national event and to an endless series of public occasions. Kahikina remembered how she hated going out in public when she was a child. Visitors to Hawai'i had somehow come to believe that it brought good luck to touch a pure Hawaiian. She hated strangers always grabbing at her, trying to touch her hair, her clothes and even her feet. She hated it. She looked out at the man again through the kitchen curtains. He must remember those things. He must know how she valued privacy. Maybe he was the Kapuahi boy, she thought, the one from Niʻihau. The family was tall and slender that way. Why won't he just go home?

Alika arrived when Kahikina finished her first cup of tea. She heard his bicycle on the back gravel path. When Kahikina's husband died a few years ago, she closed off the driveways with pass gates, strung up laser fences around her 30 acres to prevent trespassing and rarely left home. She couldn't figure out how the man got through without a passcard. Alika didn't have one. He was programmed on voice security. Kahikina thought about calling the police and having the man removed, but what if it really was him? How could she be sure? She couldn't bear more publicity, more exposure, more invasion. She asked Alika to speak to him again.

"He said he doesn't want to talk, Auntie. He said he's waiting for you to greet him."

"He trespasses on my property, uninvited and expects me to welcome him?"

"It's not his fault, Auntie." Kahikina guessed that Alika thought it was the man, the one she'd read about. And was it her imagination or did Alika say the word, "Auntie" with a hint of mockery? Kahikina looked at him in confusion.

Alika went in the house and took the laser key card from its place in the kitchen drawer. He walked to the water data board, keyed in, ran a house water treatment analysis, and began a recycling process: all waste water converted into water for the gardens. Water and land conservation had become the first priorities of the New Hawaiian Nation, and Hawaiʻi was now a world model for other island communities. Alika went next to the loʻi. He liked these taro ponds best of all with the heartshaped leaves of the plants shiny and shimmery green. He put his hand in the water near an inflow valve to check the temperature of the circulating water which needed to remain below 25 centigrade. The process of nitro-evulsion extracted liquid nitrogen from the air, making an affordable cooling agent for recycled water. Streams and rivulets now flowed freely and abundantly despite the marked increase in taro production which previously depended on naturally circulating water to maintain low temperatures. Ground water was necessary only to make up for evaporation and taro loʻi once more filled valleys and terraced hillsides. Taro, one of nature's most perfect foods. Taro, the older brother of Hāloa, the first son of the Hawaiian race. Alika looked back toward the house. Kahikina sat on the lanai in her rocker watching him.

The sun climbed through the sky, and at noon time, awakea, the world was bright. Kahikina made sandwiches and set them out on the lanai for Alika. The pitcher of water on the table dripped its transparent beads. From the kitchen, she could hear Alika come up the back stairs and leave again. Through the window, she watched him as he went around to the old man sitting under the tree. The man rested peacefully, leaning on the tree, protected from the brilliant light. Alika offered him a sandwich wrapped in a napkin. He gave him water from a cup. The tree's umbrella shade shaped them into sculptures, a dark tableau of shadows against a world of light—the old man looking up at Alika, Alika's hand held out with the cup of water, his head tilted to one side the way it does when he is intensely interested.

Kahikina turned away from the window and sat at the small table in the kitchen. Hearing Alika come back, she rose, picked up her plate of salad and moved out to the lanai. She always ate lunch with him. She listened to his reports about the plants and the grounds, and sometimes he told her things about his life outside her world, what he did, his friends, different things. He made beautiful bowls at home in the evenings, beautiful wooden bowls that he turned and polished. Kahikina imagined that the small house he lived in was illuminated by the warm colors of wood. She saw bowls like dark amber hanging from the ceilings, set up on shelves and window sills, filling up his world with the essence of trees, with the hearts of trees, making him strong. Alika has the heart of a tree, she thought, growing sturdy and full of life. On this day, they ate in silence until Kahikina finished. She looked at him and felt a pang of quick, sharp hurt.

"Why did you feed him?" As soon as the words left her mouth, she knew they were wrong, wrong words gone out, not to be taken back.

Alika stopped. He put down the cool glass he was about to drink from. He took a second to look at her making sure their eyes met. His head tilted slowly to the right and his voice was soft and silken.

"I'd do the same for you, Auntie," he said quietly.

Kahikina stood up, her face hot and flushed. She grabbed her bowl and vanished into the house slamming the screen door. She couldn't tell what he meant. Was he rubbing it in, she asked herself, or am I just oversensitive and vulnerable, seeing it everywhere? Why shouldn't I see it everywhere? God damn it, it is everywhere. At the sink, while rinsing out the bowl, she let the cold water run on her hands—water, running water to calm her down. After a few minutes, she moved into the cavernous living room where her quilt was stretched across the frame strewn with its pattern of breadfruit leaves. She sat, breathed deeply and took up the needle, moving it in and out, in and out, quilting a pattern of lines that emanated out from the appliqué, "like waves around our islands," grandma used to say.

The rhythm of the stitches began to soothe her, like chanting, like the swaying ocean, like her breath coming in and going out. She saw a day long ago. She was twenty years old, and at the medical clinic, again. Hoʻoulu Lāhui, Increase the Race, was the slogan of the project. It was an ancient slogan from another century, but now revived, it stood out, emblazoned on a holographic wall poster. In the image, the words Hoʻoulu Lāhui stretched out through a rainbow that arched over Waipiʻo Valley. Light rain fell in the valley over fields of fertile taro gently moving in a slight breeze. Under a black umbrella, two Hawaiian children meandered on the web of paths that separated the taro ponds. Raindrops swelled on the translucent leaves and rolled off. A dragonfly flew by. The sound of flowing water drifted from the poster image. It mesmerized Kahikina, making her feel peaceful and good about the project.

Dr. Haulani Haehae entered the room. She had been Kahikina's kahu ola, her personal health care giver, since Kahikina was about eight years old. Her dynamic and comforting presence gave Kahikina an immediate and almost child like sense of security. Dr. Haehae had cared for Kahikina during all her childhood illnesses. She had seen her through a difficult depression when Kahikina's mother had died, when anger and fear nearly swallowed her.

"I think of it as an act of true aloha to those who can't have children," Dr. Haehae's voice began with sincere compassion, "Just as in ancient times when people gave their children to others to be lovingly raised. And of course this project is confined to those couples in which one of the partners is of Hawaiian ancestry." The doctor brought out some papers, one of which had some population data on Hawaiians. "As you know, due to pollutants in the air, chemicals in our food and a general increase in human stress levels, by the early 21st century, infertility among the general population became a real problem. It was the same for Hawaiians as a group. We now estimate that over 50% of our couples are unable to conceive. What studies show is that while many women are able to successfully carry a child after conception has taken place, the chances for successful fertilization in many couples is slim due to low sperm count or defective ovum. In-vitro fertilization is so successful, now we can offer couples the chance to have a child of part Hawaiian ancestry, a child whose chances of growing up to be able to successfully reproduce are greater because of selectively screened fertilization. Basically we're trying to strengthen and increase the race while giving deserving couples the child they really want. Do you understand?"

"Yes," Kahikina had read all about the problem of infertility.

"I've asked you because I know your records and I know you could make an excellent contribution. Most of the donors, as you can probably guess, are only part Hawaiian. Being a full-blooded Hawaiian, your participation would be a great gift to the future."

"How will you…? I mean how does it…?" Kahikina didn't quite know the exact words for her question.

"How will it work?" Dr. Haehae smiled her reassuring smile. "The procedure takes about twenty minutes for the women. We extract ovum from you at the right time of the month just before release from the ovary, which, in your case, will be in about four days. We take the specimen, make sure it is an absolutely healthy one, and then we begin the cloning and storage processes. We expect about 300 specimens from men and women. Specimens will be matched through a random selection process that assures usage of every healthy specimen on a rotation basis so that they are all used equally."

"But you're only giving children to people who really, really want them?" Kahikina asked.

"Oh, of course, dear, a child is precious, especially one which carries our blood. Any couple requesting our help will be thoroughly evaluated."

"And no one will ever know who—"

"Absolutely not," the doctor was emphatic. "Nothing about this project will ever appear as part of public information. Our government has guaranteed the tightest security. We want to protect everyone's privacy."

Kahikina knew the New Hawaiian Nation carefully monitored the media in order, as they always said, "to avoid the self-serving and divisive confusion perpetuated on our people by the irresponsibilities of mass communication in the late 20th century." She felt confident that everything was simple and straightforward, and so she agreed to help. She was one of only thirty pure Hawaiian women of childbearing age left in the world. She had half the potential for precious human life, for full blooded Hawaiian human life. At the time, she felt a kind of obligation to participate. Dr. Haehae knew everything about her and probably counted on her to have those feelings. But this woman she thought of as a guardian and friend had lied. Had all her nurturing kindness been just to take them both together to this one day? If so, it all worked well and Kahikina had certainly done her part to increase the race. Four days after her conversation with the doctor, she had submitted to the simple procedure that sealed her commitment.

Kahikina stopped quilting and looked out at the healthy taro leaves sparkling and ripe in the sun. Rapid advances in genetic engineering had revitalized everything: beautiful crops, beautiful animals, and beautiful children, too, beautifully healthy children.

How could she have ever noticed? Two years after she had participated, she married a man in her own field of work, agricultural economics. Modeled on old fashioned home economics, they were trained to help people establish the maximum self-sufficiency in home environments. Aquaculture, productive home gardens, small scale agriculture, were all part of the home systems they designed and helped maintain. Almost too easily, she now reflected, they were offered really good government jobs in this quiet rural setting. Because of her pure ethnicity, Kahikina's eligibility for a land grant became automatic upon request after age 21. She and her husband were nevertheless astounded at the stroke of luck which awarded them through commission lottery the exquisite thirty acre parcel complete with restored historic plantation manager's house. In such an idyllic setting and engaging daily routine, how could she even have had an inkling of what might be going on? Of course it must have been part of the plan, the jobs, the house, the raises and the special new projects. They were far too clever for her. They were far too clever for everyone. Their dispersal had been so meticulously planned, everyone and everything so carefully monitored for all these years that no one ever suspected anything.

Two weeks ago, everything changed. It wasn't any expert communications saboteur that invaded the medical records to uncover the truth. It was so old fashioned, so archaic, it was almost cliché. Dr. Haehae happened to have a kind of historical nostalgia, and so, like many of her professional predecessors, she kept a personal journal, a real hand written journal in which she documented the progress of the project. In the little journal, Dr. Haehae had poured years of notes, and her own passionate feelings about her work. It lay forgotten for a long time after the good doctor died, until one day, a younger nephew came to clean and sort her belongings. That's how it all unraveled. The young man, himself a pure Hawaiian, pursued the information in the journal, relentlessly driven by the burning desire to know the names of his real biological parents.

The Minister of Health had come himself to tell Kahikina before the story became public. "I've ordered national security to delete your name and address from any and all public files. I've changed your communication numbers and covered any other possible traces which could lead strangers to you. The government is willing to provide permanent security for you for the rest of your life, but now, after what's happened, we can't guarantee complete anonymity."

"Can't or won't? You don't seem to have any trouble controlling other information." Kahikina wouldn't look at him.

"It just happened too fast. He gave out the information as if it had been approved. It's just too late." The minister paused and cleared his throat. "At any rate, the Sovereign Parliament, in a special session, asked me to tell you that Ke Aupuni Hou Hawai'i, if you would consent, would like to honor you. We would, if you agree, in a religious ceremony of the most elaborate and ancient formality, invest in you all the power of the highest, I mean the highest, ali'i. We could even establish certain kapu for you to make your life more private. We would create a special name for you and the nation would hold you always in the greatest esteem."

Kahikina continued to stare out the window.

"You see," the minister was doing his best to sound concerned and sincere, "the nation needs figures of substantial proportion, figures which in some way echo the grandeur of a great past."

"Like an invented queen mother."

He ignored her remark. "I know you need some time to think this all over. It must be quite a shock to find that your family is so, so big. I think I understand how you might feel."

Kahikina turned to him with a stare so cold he couldn't disengage from it. "Oh, I don't think so," her voice was steel. "I don't think you will ever know how I feel."

The minister left hurriedly, saying he would contact her soon.

And then two days later this man, she shook her head at the thought, this man at the gate.

Kahikina stopped to rethread her needle.

Instead of selection on a rotation basis, they had simply chosen two donations of the very best, one male and one female, both of them from pure Hawaiians. First they were cloned for grooming purposes. They removed all unhealthy traits. They altered them to withstand inbreeding. They combed through the strands of DNA, searching for and removing all defects until they were perfect. They engineered, strengthened and activated enough genetic traits from each ancestral pool to produce an infinite variety of looks. Then they cloned them again. Not once, but hundreds, maybe thousands of times. In hundreds of sterile dishes they were joined. She, Kahikina, had been joined to a man that she did not even know, a man made as perfect as herself, and thousands of pure Hawaiian children came into the world. They didn't come all at once, but were properly spaced and placed to avoid arousing suspicion. The race didn't die. It began to flourish— Hoʻoulu Lāhui.

How ironic, thought Kahikina, that my husband could not have children and didn't want to use the available alternative. How ironic that my one disappointment in life was that I never had any of my own. She sighed and lost herself in a sea of stitches. Kahikina didn't know if minutes or hours had passed before she saw Alika standing in the door with the afternoon sun behind him. In a touching gesture, he removed his hat and nervously fingered it.

"Don't stand there looking at me like that. Come inside and sit." She said it kindly.

Alika sat in his favorite chair just a little away from the one her husband always used to sit in.

"Well," Kahikina kept her eyes on her quilting. "You want me to welcome him, don't you?"

"It's not like he did anything to you."

"I never said he did," she paused. "But do the words 'violated,' 'deceived,' 'used'—do those words mean anything to you, Alika?" She hadn't intended to be close to tears.

"I'm sorry, Auntie. It's none of my business. I didn't mean to intrude on your privacy." He rose to leave, but turned at the doorway. "He's just a simple man, Auntie, mahiʻai, dirt farmer like me. He says he doesn't know what to do, where to go. I'm sorry. I just feel…I'm sorry." Alika left the house quietly.

"Don't tell mommie," grandma whispered, "Wākea was the sky father and his wife Papa was the earth. They were man and wife together; they had a beautiful daughter, Hoʻohokulani. In time, Wākea developed a great desire for his daughter, but he was afraid of Papa's anger. Wākea went to his kahuna and asked him for help. The kahuna created the kapu, all the laws which included nights, nights when it was forbidden for man and wife to sleep together. He told Wākea to go and tell Papa about these laws and to say they were declared by the gods. So on the forbidden nights, Wākea crept away to sleep with Hoʻohokulani. She had children with her father. First she bore a taro. Next she bore a man who was named Hāloa and from this man came the Hawaiian race. Papa found out about the deception and spat in Wākea's face. People today don't like this story. They don't like that it tells how our people came from a lie, a lie to deceive women, but this is the story our ancestors told, my pua."

Kahikina continued quilting until the old clock chimed four. She stretched out her legs and rubbed them before standing. Then she went to the kitchen to pour the ice tea. She poured one for herself and one for Alika, just like she did every afternoon, except when the weather was chilly, and she made hot tea instead. She started out to the table on the porch, and through the screen door. She saw Alika in the loʻi cleaning something out of the water. He looked far away and golden in the sunshine. She remembered the first day he came to work, a shy boy so eager to please. Now he was grown up, and old enough to have a family of his own. The thought that he might have been one of them was too painful to be anything but a brief stab in her consciousness. Suddenly the big house seemed very quiet and empty, just a big wooden frame yawning and creaking and growing old. Would it have been different if children had run through it? She thought of a house full of children laughing and playing and leaving trails of crumbs and toys and clothes, filling up the big emptiness of the house.

Alika examined the leaves of different stalks of the loʻi. When he moved the larger leaves at certain angles, glistening water droplets sparkled and flashed in the sunlight like a signaling mirror. He saw her on the porch and began to come toward her.

He has a nice way of moving, she told herself, quiet, sure and strong, but he doesn't really understand. He'll never understand what it's like to be forced, to have it all forced on you, forced to spawn a race against your will, without your knowledge—to be like a hole, a big gaping hole in the heavens through which thousands of offsprings pour, not one or two, not five or six, but thousands. Elements are missing here, vital, aching human elements: motherhood, pleasure, the feel of tiny feet and the closeness of small clinging limbs, the intoxicating smell of your flesh made flesh.

Alika reached the porch and sat. Kahikina poured his tea into the glass. Yes, she saw, genetic manipulation had made everything strong and beautiful, including the children, but Alika, in all his beauty could not touch this dark and wide emptiness. No one could. She sank into the white rattan porch chair watching the luminous sun in its declination.

Far away, she heard birds singing. Their songs were faint but present, somewhere on the periphery of her thoughts. Then, another sound began to rise quietly, slowly and gradually like water, like pūnāwai, spring water, seeping up from the deep ground. His voice, the voice of the waiting man, ascended through the lines of space, washed over her, crumbling gently in waves, his kāhea, calling out to be answered, calling out for recognition, flooding in the empty space and vibrating darkness. Kahikina slowly turned her face toward the sound. She rose to her feet and moved straight through the house, the fire sky behind her and fixed in her mind, warming every visible thing. Throwing open the front doors, she faced the east and her voice returned to the tall figure at the gate, making for him a deep and resonant chant of welcome.

Ke Au Ea

❧ Kanani Aton ❧

This early morning, before sunrise,
    I silently walk, naked,
    Into Waimihi
Cleanse the piko
    Body, mind, spirit
    Ho'oponopono
Spiritual renewal in the
    Sacred womb of Papa
    hi'uwai

Now, consciousness heightened,
    The wind gently pats our
    Brown faces
        Like a warm,
        Familiar breath,
            Haloa,
            Reawakening words
                dripping richly
                    from my chanting lips

Glancing upward,
           The sky's first light reflecting clouds of Kane
The cycle of life falling to
           The ground,
              Waipi'o
        The rich land
           Mauli ola ka papa honua
        The rock solid foundation to feed us

Pohaku,
 ʻai haʻa
 ʻai haʻa
  ʻai pohaku

Then sun has risen, the ceremony closing
 the last pū is sounded to the south
  Slowly, gracefully the ʻio circles above
Water sings in the ʻauwai
 E homai, E homai, E homai
 A balance struck,
  A connection made,
   a breath of life, ʻonipaʻa, ʻonipaʻa, o ʻonipaʻa

NOTES for "Ke Au Ea" provided by Kanani Aton

ke au ea: a ceremony in recognition of the 100th anniversary of the overthrow of the Hawaiian monarchy.

Waimihi: a place name for an area in Waipio Valley. An area used for cleansing.

mauli ola ka papa honua: "The rich land is forever in balance."

ʻai haʻa, ʻai haʻa: to center one's self, to balance the body by bending the knees as low as possible without lifting the ankles/heels; to hold fast and strong.

ʻai pohaku: a quote from a famous song, "Kaulana Na Pua," in defiance of the threatening forces moving in on the Hawaiian culture.

E homai: a quote from a Hawaiian chant asking the gods to grant knowledge.

I Mua e Nā Wāhine

❧ JACKIE PUALANI JOHNSON ❧

Our backs twist together, *nā wāhine o ke kai.*
We plunge our paddles as one, forcing the Pacific
Under the *'ama,* the canoe piercing the incoming swell

Salty spray clinging to lashes, lips,
Filling the bottom just enough to slow our progress
Bailer clunking between our legs, tangled,
Kahi mālie toward the horizon.

Women warriors of the waves, battling speed and
Swells that loom from the breast of an ocean *mo'o,*
Defying reason and belittling human presence.
Humbled, we push like women in labor,
Unable to stop the pulse.

There is unity in heaving with the hull.
Twisting a *haku* of bodily power with each huki,
Releasing passionate cries of effort,
No longer mothers or lovers,
But *mea hoe wa'a.*

nā wāhine o ke kai:	women of the sea
'ama:	outrigger float
Kahi mālie:	long, easy strokes
mea hoe wa'a:	canoers

❧ Appendix ❧

❧

Table of Contents by Author

About the Authors

N. KEONAONA AEA was born in Honolulu and is presently residing in Culver City, California. Among her published works are "Bearing the Light" and "Fruits Have Juice, Humans Have Blood," which have appeared in Bamboo Ridge, "Relevant Learning, Relevant Teaching," which appeared in *Kamehameha Journal of Education*, and "Trophy Room," in *The Outlook Newspaper*.

ELEANOR AHUNA was born in Keaukaha, Hilo, Hawai'i. She passed away in 2009. Her publications include Hawaiian Shores and Food, and A Hawaiian Language Beginner's Book.

KANANI ATON KELIIKOA resides in King's Landing in Hilo, Hawai'i. Her home can be found along the rugged Keaukaha coastline in a unique Hawaiian Homestead village. A mother of three children, she is the Public Information and Education Speacialist for the Department of Water Supply, County of Hawai'i. Kanani absolutely loves looking deeply into the nature of things. "For me, contemplation, observation, drifting off, returning to center, yielding a succinct verse brings satisfaction like no other."

CHERYL BAUTISTA was born in Honolulu, Hawai'i. When she submitted her poem that appears in this anthology, she was a senior at the Kamehameha Schools, Kapālama Campus. After graduation, she attended the University of Southern California in Los Angeles from which she graduated with a B.S. in Civil Engineering. She currently lives in Roseville and is working for Sundt Construction, a general contractor, as a Project Engineer. She is presently working toward a Professional Engineers License.

The recently deceased **HAUNANI BERNARDINO** was born in Honolulu, Hawai'i. She was Associate Professor of Hawaiian Language and Hawaiian Studies at Ka Haka 'Ula O Ke'elikōlani College of Hawaiian Language in Hilo. In addition to teaching, she was a vocalist, guitarist and composer of Hawaiian music. Every year on the birthday of Queen Liliʻuokalani she wrote and read a poem composed for the occasion.

PHYLLIS COOCHIE CAYAN is a native Lānaian and a descendant of one of the original families of Lānaʻi. She is a long-time community organizer and volunteer with four terms on the Oʻahu Island Burials Council, ex-officio member of Ka Lāhui Hawaiʻi, a native initiative for self governance, and a writer of grants for non-profits organizations. Previously published works include "Hakioana" in *Hawaiʻi Reviews*: Aloha ʻAina issue; "How Come You Don't Use Your Hawaiian Name?" among others, in UH West Oʻahu's literary magazine, *Westwinds*. Other works include "He lā i Kapua-a," "Echoes of Kuamoʻo," "Ancient Walls," "Ka ʻŌhiʻa Lehua," and the complete "Haikus for the Days of the Voyaging Canoes" in *ʻŌiwi: A Native Hawaiian Journal*, Vol II, 2002. In this anthology "Blue Waves..." and "All around..." were previously published as part of the complete "Haikus for the Days of the Voyaging Canoes." "Braddah" and "Pele's Last Rainforest" previously appeared in UH West Oʻahu's *Westwinds*. She is currently working on a volume of poetry to be published by ʻŌiwi in 2008-2009 as one of a trilogy of Hawaiian women poets.

DOODIE CRUZ (ERNELLE DOWNS) was born in Honolulu, Hawaiʻi and is living in Mountain View, Hawaiʻi. Presently she serves as the Information Specialist at Hawaiʻi Community College. Some of her songs, both music and words, which have been produced, are "Sittin' Around" in Acoustic Soul by John Cruz, in Smooth Jazz by Reggie Griffin, Moon Brown; "Every Child a Promise" in Keiki O Ka ʻĀina by Robi Kahakalau; "Where Are the Brothers?" in Portraits by Ernie Cruz, Jr. , more recently "Natives" and "Sweet Child of Mine" by Russell Mausa in Here I Am. The play in this anthology is her first attempt at playwriting.

MURIEL MILILANI AH SING HUGHES was born in Lahaina, Maui, and is presently residing in Glenwood, Hawaiʻi. She is a teacher at Ke Kula ʻO Nāwahīokalaniʻōpuʻu, a Hawaiian language immersion charter school in Volcano. Her poem, "Bebe You Can Be," has been published in the inaugural issue of *Meridians*, and "Hawaiians Eat Rocks" was published in Bamboo Ridge, issue #75.

CATHY KANOELANI IKEDA comes from a line of strong women writers who refuse to "sit their sadness on an elbow." Her koko iwi ʻaina hanau is in Opihikao, Kalapana on the Island of Hawaiʻi and Lahaina in Maui. With her kupuna firmly in front of her, she is able to clear the path for the generations of women behind her. As a poet, she has had her poems published in Bamboo Ridge, including some of their anthologies—*Growing up Local* and *Intersecting Circles*; however, as an English teacher at Kamehameha School, Hawaiʻi, her greatest joy is to nurture her students' own voices in their writing.

JACKIE PUALANI JOHNSON was born in Hilo, Hawaiʻi and presently resides there. She is Professor of Drama at the University of Hawaiʻi at Hilo Performing Arts Center. Along with teaching classes, she directs, produces, and acts in plays at the UHH Performing Arts Center, the Hilo Community Players, and in Kīlauea Theatre in Volcano. Previously published poems include "Edwin Soares Medeiros," "Returning Tears," "Doing Daddy's Clothes," "Kahana-side, Maui," "Walking Couplet for a Gracious Isle," "Vovo," "Ē Ka Meʻe, Ē!" and "E Ka Lālā Ola!" in *Kanilehua*, the University of Hawaiʻi at Hilo literary magazine.

MAHEALANI PEREZ-WENDT (formerly Mahealani Kamauu) has published in over a dozen literary anthologies and was a recipient of the Elliot Cades Award for Literature in 1993. Her writing reflects her love for Hawaiʻi and its people. She is a long-time political activist and has been Administrator and Executive Director of the Native Hawaiian Legal Corporation nearly 30 years. Her book of poetry, *Uluhaimalama*, in which all of her poems in this anthology appear, was published by Kuleana ʻŌiwi Press in 2007.

VICTORIA NALANI KNEUBUHL is a well-known Honolulu playwright and author. She holds a master's degree in drama and theatre from the University of Hawaiʻi, Manoa. Her plays have been performed in Hawaiʻi and the continental United States and have toured to Britain, Asia, and the Pacific. An anthology of her plays, *Hawaiʻi Nei: Island Plays*, was published by the University of Hawaiʻi Press in 2002. She is currently the writer and producer for the television series Biography Hawaiʻi. In 1994, she was the recipient of the prestigious Hawaiʻi Award for Literature and in 2006 she received the Elliot Cades Award for Literature. A mystery novel *Murder Casts a Shadow* was published in Fall 2008.

PUALANI KANAKAʻOLE KANAHELE was born in Hilo, Hawaiʻi where she is presently residing. She is Assistant Professor at Hawaiʻi Community College. In December, 2005, at the University of Hawaiʻi, Manoa graduation, she was awarded the Honorary Doctor of Letters. In 2006 she was appointed as Director of Research and Development for Hawaiian and Related Programs. She is best known as Kumu Hula, along with her sister, Nalani Kanakaʻole, of Hālau o Kekuhi, which, in September 1993 earned the most prestigious award offered by the National Endowment for the Arts in Washington, D.C., "The National Heritage Fellowship Award." In 2003, she received, along with six others, the Order of Ke Aliʻi Pauahi Award for embodying the vision of Princess Bernice Pauahi Bishop. She and her hālau gained international fame for producing and performing the epic drama *Holo Mai Pele* from the Native Hawaiian literary saga of "Pele and Hiʻiaka." After its performances in Honolulu, Maui, and in Hilo, it was premiered on PBS Great Performances. She has co-directed many other dance dramas and is sought after by many organizations in Hawaiʻi and elsewhere for her expertise as a scholar and performer in dance and chanting. Her short story that appears in this anthology is her first attempt at fiction.

RACHELLE MAIKUI (nee DUARTE), known as ʻAnakē (Aunty) Snookie by the people in Molokaʻi, was born in Līhuʻe, Kauaʻi. She is presently residing in Hoʻolehua, Molokaʻi, where she lives and works on her farm which provides food and medicine for her family. Her family consists of her partner and 15 children. Moʻomomi, whose birth is recounted in the anthology, was the third youngest child. Snookie is active in community issues and is a spiritual healer sought by people who cannot be helped by standard medicine, among others.

NALANIKANAKAʻOLE was born in Keaukaha, Hawaiʻi, as she says, "on the same lot where I was raised." She is Kumu Hula, along with her sister Pualani Kanakaʻole Kanahele, of Hālau o Kekuhi, a traditional classical dance company which are leaders of indigenous Hawaiian performing arts of hula and oli. She and her sister Pualani Kanaka'ole Kanahele produced and performed the epic hula, *Holo Mai Pele*, which toured the state of Hawai'i and was shown on PBS Great Performances. Among her published works are "Gourd Winds of Lono," in *Native Planters*, "Trails to Long Mountain," and "O Mamasan O Mamasan."

JERELYN MAKANUI-YOSHIDA was born on O'ahu and presently resides in Hawaiian Paradise Park on Hawai'i. She is married to Jay Yoshida and has three children, Kaimiloa, Maluikeao, and Kamakalehua. A graduate as an English major from the University of Hawai'i at Hilo, she is teaching at Kamehameha School, Hawai'i.

RELYN TIMBAL was a senior at Kamehameha School, Kapālama Campus when she submitted her poem that appears in this anthology. She is now manager of the restaurant China Grill Las Vegas and is living in Las Vegas.

TAMARA LAULANI WONG-MORRISON was born in Waimea, Kaua'i, and is presently residing in Volcano, Hawai'i. For a number of years she taught at various schools in the "Poets in the Schools" program. She graduated from the University of Hawai'i at Hilo with a degree in English and in Education. At present she is teaching at the Volcano School of Arts and Science, a charter school in Volcano, Hawai'i.

Student Interview of Rachelle Maikui and Comments

ON SETTING AND CONTEXT FOR "Moʻomomi"

BY FLORA H. COLLINS ON MAY 12, 1997 ❦

MY AUNTY SNOOKIE

MOLOKAʻI

For years, Molokaʻi has been known by many different names. Many of the old timers called the island Molokaʻi nui a Hina, meaning the island born of Hina, and others call it the invisible island because of the thick fog that blankets the island on many occasions.…Molokaʻi nui a Hina seems to fit it the best because of the beautiful night moon and the famous night rainbow.

From east to west and north to south, red dirt [stretches] for miles [dotted here and there] with green pastures and scattered houses. The air is hot and dry and the land is very barren, especially Kaunakakai. Hoʻolehua, where ʻAnakēʻs ʻāina hoʻopulapula (homestead lot) is located, is a little cooler than town but still filled with red dirt. [She had] been working on the land for a year now [in 1997] and [hoped] to build a home soon. The Department of Hawaiian Homelands requires a house to be built within one year of the award [but] by working on her lot ʻAnakē [fought] this and won.

RACHELLE MAIKUI, AUNTY SNOOKIE:

[When I got to the entrance of her lot] where she was pulling out the weeds outside the loʻi (taro patch), I started a chant that asked permission to enter her ʻāina. With a warm and loving smile, she quickly responded …with a welcome chant, which called out the different district names of Molokaʻi.

She said all the people in Molokaʻi know her as ʻAnakē (Aunty) Snookie; the name seems to fit her nicely. …She grabbed my hand and told me that my aura was strong and my life would be filled with happiness. …I could feel her mana as she took me to what she called her favorite place. She asked me to stand at the spot and not say a word. I stood and closed my eyes. I felt a tingly sensation all over, followed by a cool sensation; then I felt warm all over. With my eyes still closed, I began to see different visions; they were …blurry. I got scared and jumped back away from the spot and opened my eyes. "Maka'u 'oe?" (Are you afraid?), she asked me sweetly… "Anakē, what was that?" I asked. She said it was my people, my ancestors talking to me. She said that the spot I stood on was the door between the living and those who had passed, and only those with the "gift" could feel it. She told me I had the gift and I need to use it wisely. It was this gift that made the story of Mo'omomi. She feels that she is just a vehicle and things flow through her.

Mo'omomi, the Place:

The birth of Mo'omomi [which is the experience related] began at home for 'Anakē Snookie. For eight days she suffered with labor pains. The first four days were filled with visions and she begged her husband to take her to [Mo'omomi], but because the road is very rough, her husband … fought her demands. …On the eighth day the pains were really bad and when the hō'ailona [the sign] came to her, she knew she had to go there.

As we drove down the red dirt road to the entrance of Mo'omomi, I could see the difference in vegetation. The rain washes over the roadside, leaving steep pits in the road ….We stopped at the entrance of Mo'omomi and [chanted] a permission prayer before entering the area. A gust of wind welcomed us as 'Anakē blew the pū.

When the rain is plentiful, the ocean water turns dark red which encircles the island. The winds of Mo'omomi are known to be strong, which keeps the vegetation low and close to the ground. The left side of Mo'omomi is filled with sand dunes, some sixty feet high …[where] the iwi of many Hawaiians are located. Many kahunas come to the area daily to check if the bones are uncovered and need to be reburied. They have recently begun to teach the children how to perform the ceremony also. The right side is the area where 'Anakē Snookie gave birth to Mo'omomi.

Mo'omomi is known by all the people of Moloka'i. The kupunas say that it is where all the families from Ho'olehua came to spend the summer. Her story was known to all that I spoke to.

The Birth of Moʻomomi:

On the day that Papa brought her to this place, he used old netting that had washed up to the shore to build a little shack for her. She walked down the steep hill to ʻauʻau kai (bathe) before she gave birth. After bathing she walked back up to the shack where Moʻomomi was born.

From here I could see the beautiful ocean with the back drop of hills and valleys. Down at the water's edge, as I sat down to feel the water on my toes, I asked ʻAnakē for Moʻomomi's whole name. She took a deep breath, her voice became deep as she announced the whole name. At the last syllable, a huge wave rose and washed over me. "See," she said to me, "that's why I don't say his whole name often."

Student Interview of Nalanikanaka'ole and Comments

ON HER "DREAMTIME"

BY CHANDA HINA CURTICE ❧

NALANIKANAKA'OLE'S APPROACH AND GOAL IN WRITING:

Nalanikanaka'ole writes in a way that follows the Hawaiian mind flow, not only in poems that were written in Hawaiian, but the one that was "transposed" into English as well. ...She prefers to write in Hawaiian to get across ideas with as little words as possible. If not in Hawaiian, the next best thing to her would be in the style that "Dreamtime" was transposed to [where her goal is] reawakening of thought processes, Hawaiian thought processes. ...Nalani likes for her readers to read just for the effect of the imagery and what the reader herself gets from the poem.

Her main priority for writing, especially in poetry, is to write in the Hawaiian context; [for example] about things that emote timelessness, which is one of the characteristics of Hawaiian poetry.

Another important aspect to her writing is [the use of] place names. Because it was important for her ancestors to use them all of the time, she grew to like how place names were used. [You can see this in all three of her poems in the anthology.] In "Dreamtime," the different images I originally got from reading the poem [are] actual place names. [In addition to the beautiful, vivid imagery this gives at first] I discovered that the phrase "fragrant hala blooming" was referring to a place, traditionally known as Puakahinano, today known as Richardson's [an area in Keaukaha on the island of Hawai'i]. [After my interview with her] I made a weekend beach cruise past all of these places referred to in the poem and [realized] for the first time all of the hala trees at Richardson's. My eyes [were] opened to something that was there all along, but I [needed] help in truly seeing. I felt truly blessed with this new insight.

HER WRITING OF "DREAMTIME FROM THE FISHERMAN'S WOMAN"

[Nalani] started "Dreamtime from the Fisherman's Woman" about twenty years ago, at a time when people still used place names in every day context. The poem [starts by] referring to Keaukaha, where she grew up and includes a lot of memories of her own childhood. Leleiwi, the fisherman, goes out fishing, while La'ieikawai, his wife, stays ashore to gather hala. She is the fisherman's woman and this poem is told from her point of view. …She observes the dolphins making their run down the shores of Keaukaha and knows that her husband will be out all night. Lā'ieikawai, originally from Lā'ie [on O'ahu], is reminded of her childhood every time she sees her husband going out to holoholo. [In Lā'ie] it is the 'iwa birds [rather than the dolphins] that make their run. From their nests high in the cliffs of Ka'a'awa, they start their run at Ke'alohi and make their way up and down the coast, to Kahana Bay to "where the dog eyes the heavens," [popularly] known as Crouching Lion. To Nalani, these different symbols "represent the dignity of the Hawaiian mind, and how these different cycles flow." The following are the English transposed phrases and their Hawaiian place name equivalents

fragrant hala blooming:	Puakahinano (Richardson's)	[stanza 1]
yellow waters:	Wai'olena	[stanza 2]
dark waters:	Waiuli	[stanza 2]
bay of the skilled fisherman:	'Ehia	[stanza 2]
point of placed offering altar:	Leleiwi	[stanza 2]
(shelter of) the bay:	Kahana	[stanza 3]
the shining:	'Alohi	[stanza 3]

GENERAL OBSERVATION OF HER WRITING:

Almost everything she said even in the interview had kaona. I remember listening to her very carefully and then thinking I knew what she meant but not wanting to assume that my thinking was right, I would ask her, "By saying that, do you mean…?" The more I talked with her, the more I understood what it was she was saying. This is very much like hearing Hawaiian poetry in which often one must hear the poem over and over again in order to peel away the layers of kaona and gain a deeper insight into what the poem's surface does not easily reveal. … Nalani's works [as true Hawaiian poetry] have a way of saying and telling without telling, with getting across ideas using [few] words as possible…using true Hawaiian thought process.

Student Interview of Pualani Kanaka'ole Kanahele and Comments

BY LORILANI KEOHOKALOLE MAY 13, 1997 ❦

Aunty Pua, as she is known to many of us, shares her broad knowledge of Hawaiian culture in her short story. As a reader I felt drawn to this story as if my tutu were telling me a mo'olelo (story) of someone in my family.

The baby being born at home, looking for hō'ailona, family lā'au lapa'au, and denial of the first born child to a grandparent, these were real events in the Hawaiian family. [Aunty Pua wrote this story] out of her need to tell people how things continue. She shares this story as it was shared with her through her family. ...Her characters are named after place names in Hilo and Puna, areas from which her family originates and [where they grew] medicinal plants. "My family," she says, "is the source of all my work."

Aunty Pua says that when she writes, she prefers to write in Hawaiian. "I am not able to see a picture if I write in English," she said. The imagery she gets when writing in Hawaiian helps her to [recall] the past, especially when she chants or dances the hula. When writing poetry, Aunty Pua says that she likes to use few words and see many pictures. To me her Mele Ho'okipa [chant which opens the anthology] says I am the calabash. The food is all around me, in the valley, in the sea, in the sacred house of Pele, and in the forests. It is up to me to fill myself with the life-giving substance. Food may mean materials in the plant or animal form, or it may mean education and cultural/spiritual awakening.

Aunty Pua is not only a respected scholar, kumu hula, and composer, but she is a Native Hawaiian woman who creates literature in her native tongue. ... This is important because not all Native Hawaiian writers are able to do this. As a Hawaiian she shares her knowledge, continuing the cycle of learning. ...As a writer, grounded in a solid foundation with the language and traditional practices, she writes what she knows. I trust what she writes and as a reader I consider myself privileged to share her life through her compositions.

About the Editors

MIYOKO SUGANO

Emeritus Professor of English taught writing courses on computers and a variety of literature courses, in particular Pacific Islands Literature, Literature of Hawai'i, Asian American Literature, Literature of Hawaiian Women Writers at the University of Hawai'i at Hilo. Her articles on Hawai'i's local literature and on Pidgin English have been published in Meridians: Feminism, Race, Transnationalism and in Bearing Dreams, Shaping Visions: Asian Pacific American Prospectives. Her poetry has been published in Sister Stew: Fiction and Poetry by Women, and in Bamboo Ridge. Her play Issei Woman won first prize for a full length play in Kumu Kahua/UH Mānoa's Playwriting Contest for 1992 and was produced at the University of Hawai'i Theatre (now referred to as the UHH Performing Arts Center) in 1994. This anthology grew out of her joy and excitement of bringing to others the many rich voices of native Hawaiian women writers and to hear someone like Pualani Kanaka'ole Kanahele say: "I'm proud to be in the same book with passionate Hawaiian women."

JACKIE PUALANI JOHNSON

As Professor of Theatre Arts at the University of Hawai'i at Hilo, she has been directing drama at Hilo's Performing Arts Department for 30 years and has acted, directed, and sung in a number of productions both at UHH and in the community. Jackie has enjoyed teaching a wide variety of theater courses, ranging from Beginning Acting to Stage Makeup, Costuming, and Directing. Additionally, she teamed up with Miyoko Sugano to teach a learning community entitled, "Hua 'Āina: A Taste of Local Literature," in which she guided students to bring island literature to life through oral interpretation. Her recent work has centered on staging oral histories, including Kona Coffee Days, featuring the stories of immigrant farmers; Kalukalu, about historical events at the Greenwell Store in Kona; and Isabella, a one-woman show about world-traveler Isabella Bird, productions of the Kona Historical Society. Jackie is a native of Hilo. Her Hawaiian ancestry can be traced back four generations to her great-great-great grandfather, Kaiakauilani, of the Island of Hawaiʻi. A proponent of Ka ʻŌlelo Makuahine, she has three daughters, two of whom were fortunate to enjoy the fine education offered by Pūnana Leo o Hilo, Keaukaha, and Nāwahīokalaniʻōpuʻu Hawaiian Language Immersion schools. She lives in Hilo with her husband and fills her time outside of the theatre rediscovering life through her nā moʻopuna.

Glossary

Individual words, phrases, and lines in Hawaiian are usually translated into English within the line where they appear, in footnotes, or given an English version. This general glossary is provided for words that may not be defined in English or are used in unfamiliar ways. The definitions provided here were taken from Mary Kawena Pukui and Samuel H. Elberts' *Hawaiian Dictionary*, 1986 and 1975 editions. Of particular help were two appendices for the Hawaiian-English section in the 1975 edition "B. Glossary of Hawaiian Gods, Demigods, Family Gods, and a Few Heroes" and "C. Specializations of Hawaiian Gods and Important Forms They Assumed." Definitions and explanations, indicated in parenthesis, were found in *Place Names of Hawai'i* by Mary Kawena Pukui, Samuel H. Elbert and Esther T. Mookini, and in *Nā Mele o Hawai'i Nei: 101 Hawaiian Songs* collected by Samual H. Elbert and Noelani Mahoe. Other definitions were provided by former student Lorilani Keohokalole and by Pualani Kanaka'ole Kanahele. Some other terms of local variety, marked by asterisks, were gleaned from the editor's memory/reading.

'A HUI HOU!': A parting remark; "see you later."

AHU: Heap, pile; altar, shrine.

'ĀINA: Land, earth.

'ĀINA HO'OKŪ'ONO'ONO: Homestead.

ALI'I: Chief, chiefess, ruler, monarch, aristocrat.

AKUA: God, goddess, spirit; divine, supernatural.

AKULE: Big-eyed or goggle-eyed scad.

ALOHA: Love, affection, compassion, mercy; greeting, regards; sweetheart, loved one; to love, show kindness, to remember with affection; to greet, hail.

'ALOHA KAKAHIAKA': "Good morning!"

'ANAEHO'OMALU: Village, bay, and development area in Puakō, North Kona on the island of Hawai'i. Well known for spectacular petroglyphs. (*Place Names of Hawai'i.*)

'ANAKĒ: Aunty.

'AU'AU: To bathe; 'au'au kai means to bathe in the sea.

'AUMAKUA: Family or personal god; to offer grace to the 'aumakua before eating.

ʻAUWAI: Hawaiian irrigation system.

AUWĒ: Oh! O dear! Alas!

AWAKEA: Noon; to be at noon, to become noon.

ʻAWAPUHI: A wild ginger whose head on the stem was used as shampoo and whose roots were used for dye.

CAMPBELLS: Large landholder in Hawaiʻi.

HAʻIKŪ: Land division in Honomū, Hawaiʻi; land section in Kauaʻi; Land section, village in East Maui. (*Place Names of Hawaiʻi*.)

HALA: Pandanus tree or screwpine. Its leaves (lau hala), after being stripped and cured, are woven into mats, baskets, hats.

HALE: House, building.

HALEMAʻUMAʻU CRATER: Also known as the fire pit within the larger Kīlauea Crater on the island of Hawaiʻi.

HĀLOA: The progenitor of the Hawaiian race.

HĀNA: Village, bay, district in East Maui.

HANABATA: *Japanese slang for mucus from the nose.

HAOLE: White person; formerly any foreigner. Literally, hā ʻole means "no breath".

HAU: A lowland tree, the leaves are round and heartshaped, the flowers are cup shaped, the petals change through the day from yellow to dull red. The inner bark was used for rope.

HĀPUNA: Bay, beach, state park in Puakō on the island of Hawaiʻi.

HAWAIʻI KAI: A subdivision of Honolulu, Oʻahu.

HEʻE: Octopus, commonly known as a squid.

HIʻIAKAIKAPOLIOPELE: (Literally Hiʻiaka in the bosom of Pele.) Youngest and most famous sister of Pele.

HINA: Most widely known goddess or demigoddess of Polynesia frequently connected with the moon.

HIʻUWAI: Water purification festivities on the second night of the month of Welehu (near the end of the year).

HŌʻEA: To arrive.

HŌʻEA: Land section and stream, cove and land sections in Kohala, on the island of Hawaiʻi. (*Place Names of Hawaiʻi*.)

HOLOHOLO: To go for a walk, ride, or sail; to go out for pleasure, stroll.

HONUAʻULA: In this anthology, this place name refers to the Congregational Church of Kanaio and a nearby land division, Mākena, on the island of Maui.

HOʻOKUPU: Tribute, tax, ceremonial gift giving to a chief as a sign of honor and respect; to pay such tribute; church offering.

HOʻOLAUNA: To introduce one person to another; to befriend. In this anthology the word is used to introduce the works and authors to the readers.

HOʻOPONOPONO: To put to right, correct; a renewal process.

HUI: Haloo!

HULI: To turn, reverse; to curl over; to change.

HUPE: Mucus from the nose.

I MUA: Forward!

ʻIO: Hawaiian hawk, an endemic hawk found in the forests on the island of Hawaiʻi.

ʻIO LANI: Royal hawk, symbol of royalty because of its high flight in the heavens.

IPU: Gourd used as receptacles for food or water, also used as hula implements: ipu heke (gourd drum with a top section), ipu hekeʻole (single drum without a top section), ipu hula (dance drum made of two gourds sewed together).

KAHAKULOA: Land division, stream, bay, village and homesteads, West Maui. (*Place Names of Hawaiʻi.*)

KĀHEA: To call, cry out, invoke, greet, name.

KAHUNA: Priest, minister, sorcerer, expert in any profession.

KAI: Sea, sea water; area near the sea, seaside.

KA LĀʻAU: Sticks used in dancing.

KALIKO: Wild, weedy herb; used medicinally as a purgative.

KAMALŌ: Harbor, land division, village and gulch on the island of Molokaʻi. (*Place Names of Hawaiʻi.*)

KAMAPUAʻA: The "pig god," a demigod whose rootings created valleys and springs; symbol of lechery.

KĀNAKA: Plural of kanaka: Human being, person, mankind, Hawaiian.

KANAKA MAOLI: Full-blooded Hawaiian.

KĀNE: A god of creation and the ancestors of chiefs and commoners; a god of sunlight, fresh water, and forests.

KĀNEHEKILI: God of thunder.

KAPA: Tapa, as made from wauke or māmaki bark; formerly clothes of any kind or bedclothes.

KAPENA: Name of falls and pool, Nuʻuanu stream in Honolulu, Oʻahu. (*Place Names of Hawaiʻi*.)

KAPU: Taboo, prohibition; special privilege or exemption from ordinary taboo; prohibited, forbiddeokun; sacred, holy, consecrated.

KAWELU: A wind-blown grass famous in songs of Nuʻuanu Pali.

ʻKAULANA NĀ PUAʻ: "Famous Are the Children/ or Flowers" is the song of protest, opposing annexation of Hawaiʻi to the United States, by Ellen Wright Prendergast in 1893 under the title "Mele ʻAi Pōhaku" ("Stone-eating Song.") It was written after the overthrow of the Hawaiian nation.

Because a few poems in the anthology make references to the song and to "eating stones," the English translation of the song, found in *Nā Mele o Hawaiʻi Nei* is given below:

> Famous are the children of Hawaiʻi
> Ever loyal to the land
> When the evil-hearted messenger comes
> With his greedy document of extortion.

> Hawaiʻi, land of Keawe answers.
> Piʻilani's bays help.
> Mano's Kauaʻi lends support
> And so do the sands of Kākuhihewa.

> No one will fix a signature
> To the paper of the enemy
> With its sin of annexation
> And sale of native civil rights.

> We do not value
> The government's sums of money.
> We are satisfied with the stones,

Astonishing food of the land.

We back Liliʻu-lani

Who has won the rights of the land.

(She will be crowned again)

Tell the story

Of the people who love their land.

KEAUKAHA: Hawaiian homestead area, Hilo, Hawaiʻi. (*Place Names of Hawaiʻi.*)

KEIKI: Child, offspring, descendant.

KE KĀHEA: The calling, naming, greeting. In this anthology this phrase is used as a greeting to the readers, introducing the entire book.

KIAʻI: A bluff; guard, watchman, caretaker to watch, guard.

KIHAAPIʻILANI: A ruling chief of the island of Maui.

KIKAIDA: A popular Japanese adventure hero in the 70's. Kikaida had the ability to change into many forms to battle evil. (A definition provided by Lorilani Keohokalole.)

KILIHUNE: Fine, light rain, wind-blown spray, drizzle; to shower lightly.

KOHE-MĀLAMALAMA: Ancient name of Kahoʻolawe. (*Place Names of Hawaiʻi.*)

KOKIʻO: A native shrubby hibiscus.

KŌLEA: Pacific golden plover, a migratory bird which comes to Hawaiʻi about the end of August and leaves early in May for Siberia and Alaska.

KUKUI HELE PŌ: A lantern, literally light [for] going [at] night.

KULIKULI: Be quiet! Keep still! Shut up!

KŪKINI: A runner, swift messenger.

KŪPEʻE: Bracelet, anklet.

KUPUNA: Grandparent, ancestor, relative of the grandparent's generation.

LAHAINA: District, town in West Maui, formerly the gathering place for whalers and the capital of the islands from 1820-1845. (*Place Names of Hawaiʻi.*)

LAKA: Goddess of the hula.

LĀNAI: Porch, veranda.

LAULAU: Wrapping, wrapped package; packages of ti or banana leaves containing pork, beef, salted fish or taro tops.

LAUAʻE: A fragrant fern; when crushed, its fragrance suggests that of maile.

LEPO: Dirt, earth, filth; dirty, soiled.

LILIʻUOKALANI: Last reigning monarch of Hawaiʻi. She lived during the period between "early Hawaiʻi" and the United States Government Hawaiʻi; the Hawaiian Monarchial Period. (From Helena G. Allen's *The Betrayal of Liliʻuokalani: Last Queen of Hawaiʻi 1838-1917.*) She was also a writer of more than 200 songs—words and music—most well known of which is "Aloha ʻOe."

LIMU: A general name for all kinds of plants living under water, both fresh and salt.

LIMU KALA: Common long brown seaweed.

LOʻI: Irrigated terrace, especially for taro, but also for rice; paddy.

LONO: One of the four great gods, the last to come from Kahiki (Tahiti). Considered a god of clouds, winds, sea, agriculture, and fertility. Patron of the annual harvest makahiki festival. He also had the form of the pig demigod, Kamapuaʻa.

LONO MAKUA: Lono's image which was carried on tax-collecting circuits of the main islands.

LŪʻAU: Young taro tops, especially as baked with coconut cream and chicken or octopus; Hawaiian feast, named for the taro tops always served at one.

MAHIʻAI: Farmer; to farm, cultivate.

MAILE: A native twining shrub with shiny, fragrant leaves used for decoration and leis.

MAILE LAU LIʻI: One of the five forms of maile.

MAKAHIKI: Ancient festival beginning about the middle of October and lasting about four months, with sports and religious festivities and taboo on war.

MAKAWELI: Landing, land division, and river in the Waimea district on the south coast of the island of Kauaʻi.

MAKE: To die; defeated; death.

MALASADA: *Portuguese donut without the hole.

MANA: Supernatural or divine power.

MANAʻO: Thought, idea, belief, opinion.

MANAPUA: Common term used today for mea ʻono puaʻa, referring to the traditional Cantonese dumpling dim sum.

MANŌ: A passionate love; manō iʻa is an ordinary shark while a manōkanaka is a shark that is thought to be born of a human mother and sired by a shark god, or by a deified person whose spirit possesses a shark or turns into a shark.

MOANONUIKALEHUA: A goddess who came with Pele from Kahiki (Tahiti) and lived in Kaʻieʻie Channel between Kauaʻi and Oʻahu. She had two forms: one, of a woman as beautiful as a lehua tree laden with blossoms, the other of a red moano fish.

MUMU: Thud-like sound, as of footsteps.

NAʻAU: Intestines, bowels; mind, heart.

NĀPOʻOPOʻO: Light house, village, school, and beach park in Hōnaunau on the island of Hawaiʻi. The area was home to ʻUmi and Līloa, moʻi kāne of Hawaiʻi. (*Place Names of Hawaiʻi*.)

NĀ WĀHINE HAWAIʻI: Hawaiian women.

NEHE: Native shrubs and herbs in the daisy family, with yellow flowers.

NORFOLK (PINE): *An evergreen tree grown in Hawaiʻi and used by some as a Christmas tree.

NUʻUANU: Valley, park, stream, pali (cliff) in Honolulu, Oʻahu. (*Place Names of Hawaiʻi*.)

ʻOHANA: Family, relative, kin group.

ONEKAHAKAHA: Beach and beach park near Hilo, Hawaiʻi. (*Place Names of Hawaiʻi*.)

ʻŌHELO: A small native shrub in the cranberry family.

ʻŌHIʻA: ʻōhiʻa lehua refers to the flower of the ʻōhiʻa tree; also the tree itself.

ʻŌLELO HAWAIʻI: Hawaiian language.

ʻONI PAʻA: Fixed, immovable, motionless, steadfast, established, firm, resolute, determined. This was the motto of Kamehameha V and of Liliʻuokalani.

ʻONO: Delicious, tasty; to relish, crave.

ʻŌʻŌ: A black honey eater with yellow feathers, endemic to island of Hawaiʻi; now extinct.

ʻOPIHI: Limpet.

ʻŌPŪ: Belly, stomach, abdomen.

PAE: Cluster, row, group, margin or bank; level, as of a platform.

PAE ʻĀINA: A group of islands, an archipelago.

PĀHOEHOE: Smooth, unbroken type of lava, contrasting with ʻaʻā, a stony lava.

PAHU: Box, drum.

PAKA LŌLŌ: Marijuana, "pot," grass; literally numbing tobacco.

PĀKĒ: China, Chinese.

PALI: Cliff, precipice; full of cliffs; to be a cliff.

PAPA: Probably the same as Haumea, earth-mother goddess. Married Wākea, great source of female fertility; considered to be mother of Pele and of Pele's many siblings. (According to Pua Kanahele, Papa is Papahānaumoku, Earth Mother, the female entity which gives birth to all living things and is symbolic of femaleness.)

PAU: Finished, ended, completed.

PIKO: Navel or umbilical cord.

PILI: A grass known in most warm regions, formerly used to thatch houses in Hawai'i, sometimes added to the altar of the hula goddess Laka.

PO'E KAHIKO: Ancestors, 'aumakua, guardians (poe: people; kahiko: old, ancient.)

PŌHAKU: Rock, stone, tablet.

POI: The Hawaiian staff of life made from cooked taro corms, rarely breadfruit, pounded and thinned with water.

POIDOG: mongrel.

PŪ: Large triton conch or helmet shell used for trumpet; sound generated from blowing this shell.

PUA: Flower, blossom; progeny, child, descendant.

PUA KALA: The beach or prickly poppy; gray prickly plant with fragile white petaled flowers.

PUEO: Hawaiian short-eared owl, regarded often as a benevolent 'aumakua.

PŪ'ILI: Bamboo rattles, as used for dancing.

PUKA: Hole; door, gate, opening.

PUNALU'U: Land sections, gulches Honu'apo and Pāhala; harbor, landing, black sand beach and beach park and an ancient surfing area. The Punalu'u mentioned in this anthology refers to the blacksand beach on the island of Hawai'i. (*Place Names of Hawai'i*.)

PŪNĀWAI: Water spring.

PU'U: Hill, peak, cone, mound.

TI (KĪ): A woody plant whose leaves have many uses, e.g. for food wrappers, hula skirts, sandals.

TITA: Sister, *as a local slang it refers to a tough woman.

TŪTŪ (KŪKŪ): Granny, grandma; grandpa; granduncle, grandaunt, any relative or close friend of grandparent's generation. Often said affectionately.

UHIUHI: A tree with pink or red flowers and thin, broad winged pods. The wood is hard and heavy and was formerly used for sleds, spears, digging sticks and house construction.

'ULU: Breadfruit.

'UMI: Probably the most famous of early chiefs. 'Umi's time would be about 1550.

UNION MALL: One of Honolulu's main bus transfer areas, located in central downtown. (Contributed by Lorilani Keohokalole.)

'ŪPEPE: Flat-nosed.

WAHINE U'I: Beautiful women.

WAIPI'O: Valley, land section, bay, gully, stream and ancient surfing place in North Hawai'i. (*Place Names of Hawai'i.*)

WĀKEA: The mythical ancestor of all Hawaiians; according to Hawaiian tradition, a man rather than a god.

WAO KELE: Rain belt

Mele Pani
Eō Mai Ka'uku
(MELE ABOUT PLACE NAMES IN HILO)

Eō mai Ka'uku, kū hanohano a'e i ka mālie
Ka lei umauma o Hilo Palikū
Lei hiwalani i wili 'ia i ke kula o Kahuna
Līhau puni i ka makani kīhene lehua
Ua lohe ke nā kapu ahi a ka wahine
I ke one ho'i o Kaipalaoa
Pae a'e i nā ulu la'au 'ulu o Piopio
A kāu ma waena i nā lehua mamo o Ho'olulu
I ke au ka wana'ulalani e 'ō'ili mai
I ola e nā kini, i ola e nā mamo ē.

Standing stately in the calm, Ka'uku
The breast lei of Hilo at the upright cliffs
Entwined on the plains of Kahua, my sacred lei
Moistened by the rain wind lehua basket
The rumbling falls of 'Akaka was heard
From the sacred fires of the woman
To the returning sands of Kaipalaoa
Coming ashore at the breadfruit groves of Piopio
To settle among the yellow-colored lehua of Ho'olulu
In the time when the red streak in the heaven appears
Life to people, Life to children.

— NALANIKANAKA'OLE